Best Practices for Teaching with Emerging Technologies

As social media and Web 2.0 technologies continue to transform the learning trends and preferences of students, educators need to understand the applicability of these new tools in all types of learning environments. The second edition of *Best Practices for Teaching with Emerging Technologies* provides new and experienced instructors with practical examples of how low-cost and free technologies can be used to support student learning as well as best practices for integrating web-based tools into a course management system and managing student privacy in a Web 2.0 environment. "Showcase" spotlights throughout exemplify how the tools described in the book are already being used effectively in educational settings.

This thoroughly revised second edition includes

- a new chapter that explores how and why faculty are using the public web and open educational resources in place of a learning management system (LMS) and an expensive textbook
- additional tips and showcases in every chapter that illustrate faculty use of particular technologies
- the inclusion of new tools to replace technologies that no longer exist
- a revamped website featuring expanded online resources

This practical, easy-to-use guide will serve the needs of educators seeking to refresh or transform their instruction. Readers will be rewarded with an ample yet manageable collection of proven emerging technologies that can be leveraged for generating content, enhancing communications with and between students, and cultivating participatory, student-centered learning activities.

Dr. Michelle Pacansky-Brock (*@brocansky*) is a noted leader in higher education with expertise in online faculty development, course design, and facilitation. Michelle's work has helped online instructors across the nation and beyond to understand how to craft relevant, humanized online learning experiences that support the diverse needs of college students. She has received national recognition for her excellence in teaching and has held various leadership roles with the Online Learning Consortium and the EDUCAUSE Learning Initiative. Michelle is currently Innovations Lead on the Teaching & Learning Innovations team at California State University Channel Islands and the host of the HumanizED podcast. Learn more about Michelle's work at brocansky.com.

Best Practices in Online Teaching and Learning
Series Editor Susan Ko

Best Practices for Teaching with Emerging Technologies

Second Edition

Michelle Pacansky-Brock

Edited by Susan Ko

Routledge
Taylor & Francis Group

NEW YORK AND LONDON

Second edition published 2017
by Routledge
711 Third Avenue, New York, NY 10017

and by Routledge
2 Park Square, Milton Park, Abingdon, Oxon, OX14 4RN

Routledge is an imprint of the Taylor & Francis Group, an informa business

First edition published by Routledge 2013

Library of Congress Cataloging-in-Publication Data
A catalog record for this book has been requested

ISBN: 978-1-138-64364-2 (hbk)
ISBN: 978-1-138-64365-9 (pbk)
ISBN: 978-1-315-62929-2 (ebk)

Typeset in Bembo and Gill Sans
by Apex CoVantage, LLC

Printed and bound by CPI Group (UK) Ltd, Croydon, CR0 4YY

The second edition of this book is dedicated to
Michael Berman, Jill Leafstedt, Kristi O'Neil-Gonzalez,
and Michael McGarry. Thank you for your friendship,
professional support, wacky sense of humor, and picking
me up when I fall down.

Contents

Introduction

The Flipped Classroom

"Students today are unmotivated."

"Students today don't care about anything but their grades."

"Students today feel entitled and aren't willing to work hard."

Have you found yourself saying or thinking any of these things? If so, you are experiencing the effects of significant problems in higher education. This chapter will attempt to unpack statements like these by examining them within a social context and reframing them as symptoms of pervasive problems in higher education rather than an entire generation of lost souls. We will examine learning within the fabric of a society that has been transformed from the inside out by emerging technologies and ask whether or not our current learning practices are still relevant in light of these sweeping changes. To put that another way, are our students the problem? Or is it our instructional model?

This chapter serves as our initial exploration into some of the ways "emerging technologies" are reinvisioning college learning. In the context of this book, emerging technologies are defined as tools that fall into one or more of the following four categories: cloud-based applications that are easily stored online and accessible from anywhere with an Internet connection; Web 2.0 tools that make the creation and sharing of multimedia content simple; social technologies, which are tools that connect individuals and make communication an interactive process; and mobile apps, which are applications that are designed to operate on mobile devices (smartphones or tablets). The tools featured in this book have demonstrated potential to enhance college learning by making it easier for instructors and students to create and share multimedia content, build relationships at a distance, and make learning more interactive and collaborative.

As educators, it's common for us to teach the way *we* were taught, and it can be challenging to step outside of our practice to reflect on and analyze our teaching approaches. But doing so can be an enlightening experience. This book will take you for a ride through my own journey of enlightenment, which inspired me to see my teaching practices from a new perspective.

What's New in This Edition

This edition has been refreshed from cover to cover to ensure it remains relevant in light of new trends in technology. In the years following the first edition, smartphone ownership became mainstream and social media use has increased. Learning management systems (LMS) are still deeply embedded in the fabric of teaching and learning in higher education, but more faculty are identifying the potential that web-based tools hold for student engagement and learning. In light of these trends, this edition includes the following changes:

- Statistics related to technology use in this introductory chapter have been updated.
- The title for Chapter 2 has been changed from "A New Paradigm for a New Century" to "Toward Participatory Pedagogy" to focus more explicitly on teaching and learning and less on a period of time.
- Chapter 6, "Mobile and Beyond" has been replaced with a new chapter, "Unlocking Learning." This change was made in consideration of the mainstream adoption of smartphones. The new chapter was written to address the growing skepticism educators have about LMSs. The chapter examines the emerging trend of faculty who are teaching in the public web, considers how this trend impacts a student's preparedness for life after college, and critically considers the role that the open educational content may play in the future of teaching and learning.
- All chapters have been updated to include additional tips and showcases illustrating how faculty are using specific technologies in their teaching.
- New tools have been added in place of technologies that no longer exist.
- Some screenshot illustrations have been eliminated, as familiarity of particular features has increased.
- References to mobile applications and mobile learning, in general, are now baked into the chapters themselves, reflecting the mainstream use of mobile devices.
- The book's online resource site, TeachingWithEmergingTech.com, has been refreshed to include additional links and updates about tools that are sunsetting or are out of business.

From Teaching to Learning

There are particular catalysts I encountered throughout my journey that jarred me just enough to pause and consider whether or not I was doing the very best I could to meet the diverse needs of my students. One of those catalysts was an article written by Barr and Tagg in 1995, which I reflect on more deeply in Chapter 2. In their article, "From Teaching to Learning," the authors examine how our underlying assumptions and traditions inform the very outcomes of our practice. And they argue that a paradigm shift, from teaching to learning, is occurring across education. As we consider this argument more than two decades later, I think it's safe to say that the paradigm has not been dramatically transformed—but I do believe that the changes brought about through digital, mobile technologies outside the walls of our classrooms are accelerating the urgency for this paradigm shift.

Paradigm shifts can be painfully difficult, as they require a complete overhaul of the foundations that inform our processes and traditions. According to Barr and Tagg, they are most likely to occur when two indicators are present:

1. When "difficulties or anomalies begin to appear in the functioning of the existing paradigm which cannot be handled adequately."
2. When an alternative paradigm surfaces "that will account for all that the original paradigm accounts for . . . and [that] offers real hope for solving the major difficulties facing the current paradigm."[1]

I argue that low student engagement and motivation is a difficulty that college professors face as a result of using class time to deliver passive lecture content to students who are thirsty for something different. And the desire to ward off student use of mobile devices in the classroom is another difficulty that continues to create friction within the functioning of our current paradigm. Here we will unpack these difficulties by examining the way accelerated technological changes have resulted in deep-rooted shifts in generational preferences that exacerbate the way students and professors relate to college classes. We will also consider the lecture within the context of brain research and explore the ways that emerging technologies can be used to foster the type of multisensory learning that *all* of our brains crave.

Additionally, by sharing a case study from my own college teaching, I offer an alternative paradigm, the "flipped classroom"—a term that was first used by two high school chemistry teachers, Jonathan Bergmann and Aaron Sams, around 2007; became increasingly popular through the work of Salman Khan and the Khan Academy in 2011; and, more recently, has been adopted by professors around the world.[2] The flipped classroom model uses video recordings of lectures (or other online resources) that are shared with students *before* class time, freeing up face-to-face time to interact with students and apply the information learned in the videos. Ultimately, classroom time is transformed from a passive to an active experience, and the role of the instructor shifts from "sage on the stage" to "guide on the side." This chapter provides insight, guidance, and an essential toolkit for instructors who wish to get started with transforming their learning model.

This chapter is intended to open your eyes to the possibilities emerging technologies hold for changing the way college has been taught for hundreds of years and to the possible ways that instructors might transform their own teaching.

Tectonic Generational Shifts

I am a member of Generation X. I was born in 1971—the year the microprocessor was invented, Greenpeace was formed, *Ms. Magazine* originated, the voting age in the United States was lowered from 21 to 18, Walt Disney World opened, the FDA approved soft contact lenses, and the U.S. Supreme Court upheld a controversial measure to bus children in an effort to desegregate minority populations. Like you, the events and experiences of my generation played an important role in shaping who I am today.

Growing up in the heart of California's Silicon Valley, technology has always played a major role in my life. I have many vivid memories that mark some of the ways technology has influenced me. My dad had a long career as a research scientist at IBM. His home office was just below my bedroom, and late at night I would often hear a high-pitched squelch when he would dial in on his modem and connect to the "mainframe" computer. At the time, that noise was simply annoying to me, but now I can appreciate what he was doing. In the early 1980s, my dad was among the small group of American employees who continued to work from home after leaving the office. In those pre-PC days, having a computer at home was rare and having one that was connected to a network was an anomaly.

I also remember one evening when my dad called me into his office and pointed my eyes toward the large computer on his desk. He leaned toward me and pointed at a few bright green words that were moving horizontally across the black screen and said, "That's a message from my coworker." I didn't understand the complexity of that statement, but I can remember how completely stunned and exhilarated I felt as I stared at those words. "You mean, you're talking to someone on that screen who isn't here?" I asked. The prospect of communicating with another person at a distance through a computer dazzled me.

I also remember the excitement I felt in grade school when my parents rented our first VCR from the neighborhood video store. VCRs were *expensive*, and renting one for brief periods was the only way we could have the luxury of watching a movie we selected from the shelves of the video store. We lugged it home in a big black carrying case, figured out how to operate it, and huddled together on our family room sofa as we anticipated watching a movie that we selected together. And while early VCRs did have the ability to rewind and fast-forward, doing so required one to get up off the couch and manually turn the dial. And when the phone rang during the movie, our choices were to get up and answer it because it was attached to a wall (and we had no idea, by the way, who was on the other end) or just let it ring—voicemail and answering machines weren't in the picture yet.

I compare that to the context in which my own children are growing up, and the contrast is staggering. Before my husband and I made the move to DVR, my boys complained that our TV was "broken" because they couldn't rewind the shows as they watched them. Now that we have DVR, all of us have newfound expectations about watching television. We purposely avoid sitting down and watching a show at its airing time because watching advertisements is, well, a waste of time. Rather, we record specific shows and watch them at a time that fits into our schedule, which also extends the convenience of fast-forwarding through all the commercials to watch a 60-minute show in 45 minutes.

Additionally, the emergence of iPods around 2005 not only shifted the paradigm of the music industry, putting corporations (such as Tower Records, an icon of my generation) that didn't change along with the times out of business, but also dramatically altered a user's listening experience. I was in fifth grade when MTV launched. I remember sitting in front of the TV for hours waiting to see my favorite videos. My experiences were controlled by the decisions of the VJ (arguably, choices are still controlled today by media corporations, but this fact is much more less apparent than it used to be). And when my favorite videos were played, I would click "record" on my 25-pound boom box and capture the song's audio on my tape cassette. (Yes, I now realize that was copyright infringement, but I don't recall a critical discourse about this problem when I was a child.) Those cassettes were treasures to me. I took pride in the personalized music collection I had created and would scribble a customized title like "Michelle's Mix—1, 2, etc." on the front of each tape—and even make copies of the tapes for my best friends. There is no doubt in my mind that I was thirsty for personalized experiences, much like today's youth.

In contrast, there has been copious literature written about the Millennial generation, people born between 1980 and 2000 and the first generation to come of age in the new millenium. In 2016, Millennials surpassed Baby Boomers as the largest generation in the United States.[3] They also comprise the traditional college-age student population (18–24), but each year, their age creeps further and further into the age group that is considered "non-traditional." For example, in 2017, the oldest Millennials are 37 years old, and in 2015, they became the largest generation in the U.S. labor force.[4] Colleges and universities are no longer preparing for the Millennial generation. We are now having them master a set of skills they need to transition into the workplace, set themselves apart from others, and become productive contributors to society. A subtext of this book will be to ask the question, "Are the skills our students acquire throughout the path of completing a four-year degree the *right* set of skills that will support their success in a digital society?"

Data shows that there are certain trends identifiable among those in the Millennial generation. They are more skeptical than other generations, as employees are more likely to challenge the status quo within an organization, embrace lifelong learning and continue to acquire new skills, view technology as a solution, see a job as a contract rather than a calling in life, feel comfortable in times of uncertainty, see work as just a piece of what it takes to lead a fulfilling life, and they believe learning should be fun.[5] Yes, I said "fun."

The proliferation of digital technologies and, subsequently, smartphones have played significant roles in shaping these generational characteristics. Smartphones were introduced to the mainstream in 2007 when the iPhone was released and eight years later smartphone ownership was already well into the mainstream with 64% of adults owning one.[6] Smartphone ownership is even higher (85%) among Americans age 18–29, which is a critical data point to consider because smartphones are changing the way individuals connect with others, learn, and participate.[7] American smartphone owners in the 18–29-year-old age group are more likely than older Americans (age 30–49) to use their phones to get information about a job (69% compared to to 44%), access educational content (44% compared to 34%), and submit a job application (34% compared to 16%).[8] Younger Americans age 18–29 are far more likely than individuals over age 50 to use their smartphones to interact on social networking sites (91% to 55%), watch videos (75% to 31%), and listen to music or podcasts (64% compared to 21%).[9]

Individuals who come of age in our mobile, digital world develop social groups by interacting with individuals in both the physical and online realms. For example, my son, who is 14 at the time of writing, and lives with me in California, regularly plays Minecraft, a popular online video game, with people he calls his friends who live in Australia and New Zealand. He's never met these people in person, but he speaks with them regularly on Skype and connects with them on Snapchat. The point here is that "online" is a *culture* to young people. Yet to most colleges, *it is a delivery method.*

Digital and mobile technologies provide young people with rich options and highly personalized, community-oriented experiences. As such, Millennials are more likely than older generations to want to understand why they are asked to engage in an activity and may seek out clear expectations in advance. I am familiar with the tension these characteristics can cause in college classrooms that are founded on a top-down hierarchical model in which the professor dictates what students will do, and the students are expected to be quiet and do it. This is one of the reasons Chapter 1 of this book includes tips for cultivating a community-oriented classroom.

Let's take this one step further and take a peek at the generation following the Millennials, about which generalizable data does not yet exist since they have not entered the consumer or job market. My two children are both members of the post-Millennial generation—a generation that is yet to be named (but one early suggestion is the "Homelanders").[10] They are the first generation to be raised within a truly digital, mobile society, and while we cannot identify their unifying characteristics yet, Common Sense Enterprises predicts that they will likely be the most "racially and culturally diverse generation in US history" and because of "advances in global communication, they may be the most transient generation as well."[11] This generation arrives on university campuses in 2018.

My "post-Millennial" children, born in 2000 and 2002, received their own iPod between the age of seven and eight and their first smartphone upon entering middle school. An iPod, which seems like an antique relic, held thousands of songs, all selected by the owner. The iPod was also the first instance of mobile entertaining, as it held TV shows, full-length movies, audiobooks, and digital pictures—and later versions eventually included a video camera too. iPods amazed me. All that functionality contained in a package that was smaller than the comb I used to carry in my back pocket in middle school.

The iPod was the first technology to begin to resculpt the meaning of "personalization" to this generation (I didn't mention that each of my boys had an iPod in their favorite color too). And smartphones? Well, they are in a league of their own. A smartphone is, essentially, an iPod with an Internet connection, voice and text communications, robust still and video camera, and a collection of social and entertainment-based apps, curated by the owner. They are not "phones" to my kids. They are devices that they use every single day to document and share their experiences and stay current with the lives of their friends. Their phone is never far away. In fact, a 2010 study found that 90% of Americans age 18–29 sleep with their phone.[12]

Ask yourself this: if your earliest music experiences involved the option to curate your very own audio and video collection and you had access to it at any time and in any place, would you be as motivated to sit by the radio and listen to songs *someone else* has decided to play for you? That's very similar to the motivation and engagement problem we have in college today. It's not that students aren't willing to work hard—I just don't believe that. I've seen amazing passion, dynamism, and effort in my students' work, and I've seen glazed, detached stares—the difference resides in the type of learning environment I use to engage them.

Julie Evans is the director of Project Tomorrow, a non-profit organization that facilitates the annual *Speak Up* survey, which tracks and analyzes trends in K–12 student learning by surveying nearly 300,000 students each year. Since 2005, the survey has had its finger on the pulse of student use of technology and its correlation with learning preferences. In 2005, according to the survey, half of the sixth graders who were surveyed owned a cell phone (that is, a mobile phone without a connection to the Internet). In 2010, that statistic held true, but an additional one-third of them owned a smartphone. In 2015, 86% of high school students, 72% of sixth to eighth graders, and 46% of third to fifth graders used a smartphone.[13]

Mobile device use is changing how students interact with their teachers and each other. In 2015, about half (47%) of ninth to twelfth graders said they used Twitter, which is an increase from just 11% in 2011. Also, 27% of students in grades K–12 said they regularly watch videos created by their teachers. Smartphone use by students is also increasing student-teacher contact outside of class: in 2015, 48% of students interacted with their teachers via email and 15% through text messaging. Not surprisingly, students are thirsty for more integration of mobile devices into the classroom. Seventy-six percent of students think every student should have access to a mobile device during the school day to support learning.[14]

Administrator attitudes and policies about the role of smartphones in the classroom are changing in K–12 education. In 2010, the majority (63%) of principals felt it was not likely that their students would be allowed to use their own mobile devices at school. In just three years, that number decreased to 32%—almost in half! In 2015, 41% said they were likely to allow students to use mobile devices at school, and 10% said they already allow students to use mobile devices in class to support learning activities. Further, most parents (60%) of students in K–12 education would like their child to be in a class that allows students to use their own mobile devices.[15]

K–12 educators are exploring the possibilities of these shifts, particularly students' growing demand for "untethered learning," defined as learning that occurs from anywhere at anytime, and it's directly correlated with the widespread use of mobile devices. Online classes are now offered at more than 40% of high schools to provide remediation, provide an alternative pathway to stay in school, and provide options for credit recovery. Teachers of these online classes note that technology can help students understand how to apply academic concepts to real-world problems, take ownership of their learning, and hone problem-solving and critical-thinking skills. Considering these K–12 trends provides college educators with a new lens through which to consider poor student engagement in higher education.

The Engagement Problem

Back in 2006, a student of mine approached me after class one day and asked if I had heard of a website called YouTube. When I said no, she went on to explain to me that it's a website that allows people to upload videos and share them with each other. I can remember thinking, "So? Why on earth would people want to watch other people's videos? How is that revolutionary?"

At the time of this writing, YouTube has more than a billion users. Every day, people around the world watch hundreds of millions of hours of video on YouTube. More than half of all YouTube views come from users on mobile devices, and the average viewing session on a mobile device is more than 40 minutes.[16] I guess it's safe to say I was wrong.

Outside the walls of the classroom, most college students learn through connected and highly personalized experiences. Millennials are accustomed to learning from their peers in a virtual community in which their opinions and ideas matter. This model dramatically contradicts the traditional, hierarchic, top-down model imposed in most college classrooms. If technology can deliver the same message in a better, more personalized, convenient way—that meets not only the preferences of a student but also his/her individualized learning needs—then why are we not exploring or at least contemplating this as an opportunity to transform teaching and learning?

Howard Rheingold, professor at Stanford and Berkeley, author of several books, including *Smartmobs*, and the creator of the *Social Media Classroom*, has influenced my thinking about the significance of teaching with social media. I had the opportunity to meet Rheingold at a conference in 2010, but he influenced me long before that through the videos he openly shares on YouTube. I have enjoyed listening to his presentations on my iPhone during my routine walks through my neighborhood. Early on, his messages about the importance of cultivating a "crap detector" in our students resonated with me. To summarize Rheingold, a "crap detector" is the ability to discern valid digital content from meaningless, well, crap. He's right—and, yet, where are our students learning this skill? In the era of "fake news," the need for this skill is more fundamental than ever.

The other Rheingold message that has stuck with me most is his willingness to be blunt about the purpose of a face-to-face college class. Rheingold says,

> I ask [my students] on the first day of class, why are we standing here? Why do we all come to this physical place? Do you rush home at 7:00 at night to watch your favorite TV show or do you record it?

Rheingold is reshaping his teaching paradigm to align with the expectations of his students but also to make the time he spends with them more effective and productive. He continues, "[I]f I have an hour's worth of lecture, as teachers have had for the past thousand years, I'll put it on YouTube which has not existed for a thousand years."[17] By recording his lecture content (with a simple webcam and a free YouTube account) and sharing it with his students prior to class, he "flips" his classroom from a passive to an active experience. Rheingold is, by no means, the first or only educator to use the flipped classroom model; he's one of the many experimenting with the concept. In a flipped classroom, coming to class on Tuesday and Thursday for an hour and a half becomes an active experience that is grounded in discussion, debate, and analysis, rather than 90 minutes of passive listening.

If you have felt like your students do the minimal work they can just to get by and get a good (or decent) grade, you're right. But this is partly because we have constructed a model that enables them to do so. Imagine a different paradigm—one like Rheingold's that uses emerging technologies to have students watch your lectures online (from a laptop, phone, or tablet) and complete a formative assessment before coming to class. One in which you could review the results of the formative assessment and then make a list of proficiencies that have not been mastered and use class time to work through them actively with your students. *Why do we not do this?*

Michael Wesch, an anthropology professor at Kansas State University, who was named 2008 U.S. Professor of the Year by the Carnegie Foundation for the Advancement of Teaching, is, perhaps, best known for his 2007 video "Visions of Students Today" (which, at the time of writing this, has received 4.5 million views on YouTube). The video pans through a large lecture hall and zooms in on the wall, which reveals a handwritten question, "If these walls could talk, what would they say?" Then individual students reveal brief written messages to the camera. One says, "My average class size is 115." Others reveal, "18% of my teachers know my name," "I buy $100 text books that I never open," and "When I graduate, I will have a job that doesn't exist today." The five-minute video paints a picture of college learning as irrelevant and ineffective at meeting the future goals of 21st-century students.

Both Rheingold and Wesch see the possibilities that emerging technologies hold in reshaping college into an experience that actively engages students in their learning, puts them in the driving seat, and fosters the critical-thinking skills necessary for 21st-century success.

Brain-Friendly Learning

 Another benefit of teaching with emerging technologies is the potential they hold for crafting multisensory learning experiences, which are more akin to the way the brain is wired to learn. Teaching to support the way the human brain works? What a concept! John Medina, an affiliate professor of bioengineering at the University of Washington School of Medicine and director of the Brain Center for Applied Learning Research at Seattle Pacific University has extracted the essentials of decades of brain research and compiled what we know about how the brain learns into 12 concise rules. Published in text format as a book titled, *Brain Rules*, and communicated in true multisensory fashion online at http://brainrules.net, Medina's modules serve as a clear, concise guide to illuminate just what's so backward about formal education. Medina argues that, as a society, we "ignore how the brain works" and the only scandal is "why we're not fixing it." In fact, if you were to envision a large group of students sitting passively in a classroom listening or writing for long periods of time, you would be picturing an "almost perfect anti-brain learning environment," according to Medina.

Here are three of Medina's "brain rules" that are relevant for 21st-century college educators and a few of my own thoughts about how emerging technologies can assist us with developing more brain-friendly learning.

Exercise Boosts Brain Power

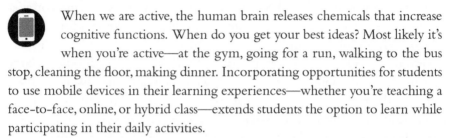 When we are active, the human brain releases chemicals that increase cognitive functions. When do you get your best ideas? Most likely it's when you're active—at the gym, going for a run, walking to the bus stop, cleaning the floor, making dinner. Incorporating opportunities for students to use mobile devices in their learning experiences—whether you're teaching a face-to-face, online, or hybrid class—extends students the option to learn while participating in their daily activities.

Mobile content has potential to transform passive listening into an experience that can be engaged during physical activity. Imagine if lectures were assigned to students as homework and students could listen to them on a mobile device. Do you think they'd sit in one spot and listen? That certainly would be an option, and one way to make a long commute more productive, but it also opens up the opportunity to listen while out for a jog, walking the dog, cooking dinner, or vacuuming the floor.

Sensory Integration[18]

Imagine a picture of a brain. When that brain is exposed to each of the five senses—seeing, hearing, listening, tasting, and smelling—a different region of the brain is activated. The more senses that are engaged in an experience, the more a brain is stimulated and the longer a person remembers what has occurred. Simply, if you were a student in a class listening to a professor, you'd remember less than a student in the next class listening to the same lecture supplemented with images, and even less than a student sitting in a third classroom who was listening to the lecture, viewing images, and stimulated with text. Unisensory learning never beats multisensory learning.

This is compelling for many reasons. All of us (not just traditional college-age students) are now able to learn through video, images, and text, and many of us can do so using the mobile devices in our pockets. The tools to create multisensory learning have never been more accessible to the general public, and using them no longer requires one to be a multimedia production expert. If we're serious about learning, this is the brain rule we will take seriously.

Vision Trumps All Other Senses[19]

 Each of the senses enhances learning, but the human brain particularly loves images. Humans are visual creatures. We began creating visual representations of our world tens of thousands of years before we devised written languages. Referencing brain research from the 1960s, Medina lucidly states, "Hear a piece of information, and three days later you'll remember 10% of it. Add a picture and you'll remember 65%." This is the underlying reason why advertisements are visual!

In contrast, when most college professors employ a "visual" teaching aid, they're usually inclined to develop a PowerPoint presentation. PowerPoint certainly has the potential to create a compelling visual experience. However, rather than using PowerPoint to craft a dynamic visual backdrop to a verbal presentation, most of us fill the slides with text.

Medina's advice is to delete your PowerPoints and create new ones. That is one approach, but there are many other tools that foster visually centric content creation, capsizing the traditional hierarchy of text to image (see Chapter 4 for tips!).

Our recent shift from a mechanical, industrial to a digital, information society has resulted in extreme shifts in preferences and expectations, a reconceptualization of the most effective use of face-to-face time for teaching, and advances in cloud computing and audio-visual technologies have yielded easy to create, multisensory experiences that support the way the human brain is wired. These three elements will continue to shake the foundation of the traditional "instructional" paradigm in which higher education is rooted. We have two roads ahead of us and only one leads to a truly transformed paradigm. Which is your path?

Putting It All Together—A Flipped Classroom Experiment

Between 2006 and 2009, my online classes went through a transformation. An arduous recovery from open-heart surgery in early 2006 left me with much time to spare and reduced physical capacity. While I didn't know it at the time, within the coming months, the Internet as I knew it would be revolutionized and transform from a static information repository to an interactive authoring platform facilitating dialogue and connections between people anywhere in the world. This was the dawn of Web 2.0, one of the most provocative social shifts brought about by technology since the introduction of the printing press.

Before my eyes, blogs began to appear everywhere and podcasts were all the rage. Everyone and anyone now had an open invitation to become an author. In that time frame, I spent a lot of time walking, and rather than listening to music, I began to listen to educational podcasts and archives of conference presentations. Within a very short period, I was amazed at how much I had learned from scholars and thought-leaders who had shared these simple audio files. This was a profound moment for me.

I remembered sitting in my office with one of my students the semester prior and feeling agitated that he was rude enough to keep one iPod bud inserted in an ear while having a conversation with me. Those damn iPods were every-where, and they were "distracting my students," I thought. But then I saw things differently. I understood the possibilities hidden in the popularization of iPods. It could be a tool I could use to share content with my students and empower them to learn from anywhere.

So I learned how to create podcasts and then leveraged each of the written lectures I had composed for my online classes as transcripts and turned each of them into a podcast episode. I originally hosted these on a personal site, as my institution did not provide me with an online hosting option, and linked them into my learning management system for students to view online or export onto their iPods for a mobile learning experience. But I didn't get rid of the written lectures; instead, I provided both options to students and let them guide their learning and choose the format that worked best for their unique needs.

The second significant change I made was the integration of VoiceThread, a tool that enables online conversations in voice, video, or text around media, into my online classes. As an online art history professor, I was challenged to meet my pedagogical goals within the text-dominant learning management system I was using. I could sense that the text-dominated discussion forums were not effective in achieving my course's learning objectives. I needed an environment that could con-nect students with images and allow them to visually analyze a painting while com-menting on it—something that just doesn't happen fluidly in a discussion forum. When I saw the VoiceThread interface, I knew I had found what I was seeking. VoiceThread creates a conversation space centered around slides that each contain a piece of media (an image, presentation slide, video, document, etc.). The conversa-tions are asynchronous (time shifted), allowing users to collaborate at a time that is convenient for them, and comments may be left in text, voice (with a microphone or a telephone), or in video with a webcam or smartphone via the mobile app.

I am often asked, "How do you find out about all these different tools?" Well, through my participation in social media. In 2006, I learned about Voice-Thread from a blog post written by Beth Harris, who is now employed as a dean at the Khan Academy after spearheading the creation of Smarthistory, a compelling open educational alternative to a traditional art history textbook, with her colleague Steve Zucker. I commented on Beth's blog, thanking her for sharing VoiceThread with me. Within a very short time, Beth wrote back and asked me if I'd like to collaborate on a VoiceThread.

Within a day, she created a new VoiceThread that included several different views of a 15th-century Flemish painting, *The Arnolfini Portrait*, by Jan van Eyck. Beth left the first comment and then emailed me to let me know it was my turn. Later that day, I clicked on the link to the VoiceThread, logged into my account, listened to her comment, and left a voice comment in response to hers. We continued our back and forth dialogue for the first couple of days, at times that were convenient for both of us (she is in New York and I'm in California). Then Beth invited two colleagues of hers to join us, art historians from the East Coast. We continued with a discussion about the painting, applying our own perspectives and a variety of art historical methodologies. The collaboration was not only fun and inspiring for me but also actually produced a collaborative learning resource that I shared with my students in future semesters. This product allowed for my students to listen in on a conversation between a group of art historians about a painting—so much richer than having me lecture to them about it! You can view the collaboration here if you're interested: http://voicethread.com/share/3511/.

Participating in that collaborative VoiceThread with Beth and her colleagues was pivotal for me. It put me in the seat of both a *teacher* and a *learner*. It opened the blinds and showed me how easily I could collaborate with others, at a distance, in voice and video (and for free). It gave me confidence and helped me understand that even though I was an art historian, not an audio/video web specialist, I could find tools that enabled me to convey my social presence to my online students and offer new, exciting pedagogical models.

I reflected deeply on the provocative shifts in learning that were occurring in my life as a result of emerging technologies and, little by little, began to reconstruct my online classes. Why my *online* classes and not my *face-to-face* classes? That's a great question. Probably the best answer is simply because it felt most natural to me to embrace web-technologies in my web-based classes. By mid-2007, I had transformed my online classes by integrating podcasts, VoiceThreads, and pulling students into a media-rich blogging experience in Ning. (Ning provides a method for anyone to create a private social network. At the time it was free, but now it's a premium tool.) I felt like a chef who had been granted a new spice rack filled with magical seasonings. My students' feedback exhilarated me, and the high level of student participation was enough to make me pause and realize *there is a better way of doing things.* Ironically, I was surrounded by a deeply concerned institutional discussion about low online success and retention rates, while mine had steadily increased to over 80%.

That year, I was honored with the Sloan-C Excellence in Online Teaching Award (Sloan-C was rebranded as the Online Learning Consortium or OLC in 2014). This was an important moment for me. Like many (most?) professors, I was teaching in solitude, making changes and revisions to my courses within a vacuum. As much as I wanted to peek at what others were doing so I could learn from them and share my own work, I didn't have a context to do so. I was excited about my online classes and was thirsty to be part of a community focused on exploring the meaning of "quality online teaching," rather than dwelling on what's wrong with online classes.

Receiving the Sloan-C Award empowered me because I was able to have my courses evaluated within the context of a national conversation about quality online learning and, as a result, I felt more confident and began to share what I was doing with other educators. In 2007, I began my own blog and started to share my ideas and my students' feedback with the global educational community. That would be my path to finding the community I had been seeking. Sharing became my fuel for my own lifelong learning—a way for me to give back to a community from which I had learned so much. And the more I contributed, the more I gained through the connections I made.

While the engagement and learning in my *online* classes soared to new heights, my *face-to-face* classes had changed very little. They still, for the most part, consisted of lectures with some online assignments (view this movie, review this website, etc.). I felt an increasing tension each time I delivered a lecture in person that I had already developed as a mobile podcast episode. "Why am I doing this?" I would ask myself.

For a long time, I struggled to figure out how to make sense of the problem. My internal dialogue went something like this, "I'm lecturing to my students. I'm spending my time with them to deliver the same information I have recorded as audio podcasts. This feels redundant. But if I give them access to the mobile lectures, they won't come to class. Why should they? But why should I lecture to them when this information is available in a method that will likely help them learn more effectively by extending the option to pause, replay and rewind?" I was stuck and didn't know what to do.

I also felt frustrated with my students' passivity. Online, my students were participatory and interactive. Offline, most of them would enter class, recline in their seats, and stare at me with glazed eyes. I'd spend my time with them fighting to keep them engaged—breaking up long lectures with video clips, small and large group discussions, using writing prompts—and these things helped but they were by no means "transformative." I now know I was tinkering around the edges and avoiding the heart of the issue. If I really wanted to address the problem of low student engagement, I had to take a risk. I had to transform my paradigm.

So in spring 2009, I made a drastic change in my History of Women in Art class. I stopped lecturing in class. It was a frightening feeling to imagine spending 16 weeks with my students without lectures to deliver. Lectures are how I was taught art history, and they are the only way I had ever taught it (in a physical classroom). What would I do with my students? What if they didn't participate? What if they didn't do the work? There was only one way to find out.

I revised my syllabus to communicate my student expectations, and I carefully wrote a new class philosophy that emphasized the central role of community. I explained that a community is based on giving and taking, and students would learn greatly from one another's contributions. I also communicated our new model to my students *before* the semester began. I expected that my innovative model might not appeal to some students, so I sent out an email a week prior to class starting (using my course management system), attached the syllabus and included a personalized letter explaining my intent and how the class would differ from a "typical" college lecture class.

As I created the plan for the semester, I found myself adopting much of the instructional design of my online class. The course was organized into modules that lasted one week on average. Each module included "pre-class" as well as "post-class" assignments. The pre-class assignments were due prior to the first class meeting for that particular learning module. They included a description of the unit, a list of learning objectives, a reading assignment, a lecture—which I shared as an illustrated PDF and an enhanced podcast (my voice narration synced to still images), giving students a choice as to which one to access—and a VoiceThread.

The pre-class VoiceThread served a couple of purposes. First, it was a formative assessment. I designed it around prompts that were aligned with the learning objectives for that particular unit. The students needed to complete the reading and lecture to be able to make meaningful contributions in the VoiceThread—again, given a choice—in either voice, text, or video format. The formative assessment gave students an opportunity to summarize and apply what they had learned from the reading and lecture. But each VoiceThread was also a participatory environment. Students were required to access the activity and leave a specific number of comments, but they were also able to listen to and read comments left by other students, creating a contextual framework in which students could learn from one another.

Prior to the first class meeting for each new learning module, I spent about 45 minutes in my office listening to and reading the comments left in the VoiceThread. Traditionally, this would be time I'd spend preparing to deliver a lecture. Instead, I was assessing my students' understanding of core concepts and mentally preparing myself for an hour and a half of discussion and activities.

As I reviewed the VoiceThread, I took detailed notes as I listened and read. I made charts that listed outstanding student contributions, identified topics that were mastered by the group, and highlighted areas that needed additional attention or held potential for deeper discussion. Then, when class started, I turned on the computer and projector and displayed the VoiceThread, which was simply accessed through a link in our learning management system, on the screen. I referred to my notes and began to facilitate a discussion about the VoiceThread contributions—pulling individual students into the conversation by name. This naturally took the class into a thoughtful dialogue, providing me with ample opportunity to applaud outstanding student work, prod students with Socratic questioning about comments that needed further explanation, encourage students to make deeper connections and engage in debate when conflicting ideas surfaced, and, ultimately, use the class time to fulfill the needs of the group and spend more time fostering critical-thinking skills.

In addition to facilitating the VoiceThread discussions in person, I spent most of the rest of our class time having students work in groups to analyze and discuss image comparisons—the quintessential art history summative assessment that engages higher order thinking skills that can be challenging for students to foster with little to no opportunity for practice. We also debated, discussed, and questioned topics together, referenced relevant current events, took a field trip to a local woman artist's studio, and watched a full-length feature film about the life and art of 20th-century painter Alice Neel (which was our only truly passive in-class learning experience, but was followed by a very emotional discussion fueled by the strong sense of community fostered in the group).

The post-class assignment in each learning unit included a second unique VoiceThread that was designed around a second set of prompts that demanded higher order thinking skills. The slides in these VoiceThreads were more heavily focused on image comparisons in which students would be asked to contribute unique ideas as well as build off of the ideas of students who commented before them.

Throughout the semester, there were also three summative assessments, which involved a long take-home essay that required students to select from one of several prompts focused on comparing and contrasting two images and an in-class, multiple-choice and short-answer test.

At the end of the semester, I conducted a simple survey using the survey tool within Blackboard—77% of students responded. I also invited students to my office to discuss their experiences. Three students came to speak with me and, with their permission, I recorded our 20-minute discussion (which has been shared on my blog ever since and is shared as a link in the book's online resources, see the final chapter).

The survey results revealed increased student satisfaction, engagement, sense of community, and critical thinking. Despite the fact that 81% of students strongly agreed or agreed that the flipped classroom model required them to spend more time on homework assignments, 97% strongly agreed or agreed that the class was a successful learning experience. Additionally, when comparing the new flipped model to a traditional lecture class, 81% of students strongly agreed or agreed to the following: the new model was a more enriching learning experience, they had more opportunities to ask questions in class, their ideas and perspectives mattered more, and class time was more relevant to their needs. Also compelling is the fact that 89% of the students who responded strongly agreed or agreed that the flipped classroom experience required more critical thinking than a traditional lecture class.

While from afar it may seem that technology is at the core of the flipped classroom model, I would argue differently. The foundation of success is a clearly structured instructional design model that organizes content into learning modules, each aligned with a series of measurable learning objectives and a continued focus on modeling the importance of community. Also critical is the need for an instructor to make the intrinsic shift from "sage on the stage" to "guide on the side," or, to reference Barr and Tagg again, from an instructional to a learning paradigm.

College students are trained to expect a classroom environment that is designed around a hierarchy that places them at the lower level and their instructor above. This implicit structure informs everything about the way a student relates to the class—where they sit, how they prepare, and their attitude about the semester. Think about the physical organization of a classroom—desks organized around a single expert, sometimes even in an elevated "theater" style. The messages that are implicit in the physical organization of a typical college classroom must be deconstructed for a flipped classroom to be successful.

Therefore, when an instructor embarks upon an instructional model that assumes a flattened relationship between student and instructor, like the flipped model, this must be communicated and discussed so it's clear to students. The "sample class philosophies" shared in Chapter 1 are an effective first step for setting the tone. But the success will rely on consistent activities in and out of class that model a community of learners who are expected to share and learn together.

The flipped classroom opens the door to new possibilities for college learning models. It puts students in control of their learning and also gives them a chance to learn how they learn. As one student in my class responded, "I honestly thought that I would not like . . . it; I thought it would just add more work. After completing the course, I think that it actually helped me more than hurt me . . . I truly think that it has helped me learn better."

And that was the unexpected outcome of the class, for me. Originally, I began integrating audio podcasts and PDFs for lectures in my online classes in an effort to keep my content Americans with Disabilities (ADA) compliant—so deaf students could have the option to read. But what I didn't realize was how valuable these options were to *all students.* Amazingly, at the end of the semester, when I surveyed my students, I learned that when they were given the option to read or listen to a lecture, 40% chose to read, 15% chose to listen, 30% did *both* at the same time, and 15% toggled between the two throughout the term. Now take a step back and think about those statistics. In a traditional college classroom, a student's only option is to listen—yet when given a choice, it was the *least utilized method.*

For me, this experiment illuminated a whole new way of thinking about college teaching. It has encouraged me to rethink our age-old ways of doing things and understand that our technologically rich society holds opportunities for making learning more effective, more inclusive, more engaging.

Problem or Opportunity?

I have shared my personal story with you to provide a practical example of how emerging technologies can be used to transform college learning but also as a way of reframing the student engagement "problem." It's true that today's students *are* different but they've changed only because of the deep-rooted shifts that have occurred outside the walls of our campuses. Technology should *not* be integrated into college learning for the sake of using cool new tools to engage tech-savvy students. Beyond the boundaries of our college campuses, technology is the driving force that has shifted our society to a highly collaborative, participatory model. And within our classes, using it in support of a course's learning objectives is one way we can make our students' learning more relevant, more supportive of diverse student needs, and more engaging, as well as prepare them for a successful life in our digital, interconnected, collaborative society.

By no means is my "flipped classroom" an example of the *best* way to modify our teaching practices with emerging technologies. Rather, it is offered as a *possible* way to change the course of college learning. Sometimes we can feel the need for a change, but it's not until we "see" an example that the ideas start to flourish and new paths open in front of us.

This chapter serves as our first step into the depths of a rich, complex topic. Each reader of this book has his or her own objectives, and it is my hope that this book will meet them, in addition to piquing your curiosity to try something new and inspire you to see technology in a new way. As the lives of our students continue to be transformed by social, mobile technologies, we have uncharted territory in front of us. As we struggle to fend off the distractions of Facebook and texting in our classrooms in an effort to sustain our traditions, are we missing something grand? Something dazzling? We will never know if we don't pause and reframe our problems as opportunities.

The following chapters will provide you with more practical strategies through a cascading array of "showcases" from real college classrooms emphasizing how emerging technologies are reinventing college learning. As noted earlier, this book defines "emerging" as technologies that have made a splash in college learning but have not yet been adopted into mainstream teaching. The professors showcased in this book represent the diverse realities of college teaching. They come from two-year and four-year institutions, some with no instructional support, some with a robust team. Some teach full time and others teach part time (sometimes at more than one institution). But what they all share is the willingness to step outside their comfort zone and take a risk to improve a problem. Teaching with emerging technologies involves stepping outside the traditional guise of subject-matter expert and taking on the role of a learner.

The next chapter will provide you with several key strategies and techniques for making the shift to a student-centered class including writing your class philosophy and establishing the foundations of a community-oriented learning environment. From there, in Chapter 2, we'll continue to investigate the paradigmatic shift toward participatory pedagogy and discover strategies for evaluating emerging tools; in Chapter 3, we'll peek inside the "essential" toolkit that is a must for all professors using emerging technologies in their classes; in Chapter 4, we'll examine audio and video tools for bringing your human presence into your online course content; in Chapter 5, we'll review participatory tools for collaborative learning and producing student-generated content; and, in Chapter 6, we'll delve into the fringes of higher education and take a look at the experiences of faculty and students who are pushing the LMS and expensive textbooks aside to teach and learn in the public web with open educational resources.

Notes

1. Barr, R. B. & Tagg, J. (1995). From Teaching to Learning—A New Paradigm for Undergraduate Education. *Change Magazine*, 27 (6): 12–25.
2. For more information about the history of the term "flipped classroom," visit http://blendedclassroom.blogspot.com/2011/05/history-of-flipped-class.html.

3. Fry, R. (2016, April 25). Millennials Overtake Baby Boomers as America's Largest Generation. *Pew Research Center*. Retrieved on September 17, 2016 from www.pewresearch.org/topics/millennials/.

4. Fry. R. (2015, May 11). Millennials Surpass Gen Xers as the Largest Generation in the U.S. Labor Force. *Pew Research Center*. Retrieved on September 18, 2016 from www.pewresearch.org/fact-tank/2015/05/11/millennials-surpass-gen-xers-as-the-largest-generation-in-u-s-labor-force/.

5. Wendover, R. W. (2016). Succession Planning and the Emerging Generations: Nine Trends You Need to Know. *Common Sense Enterprises, Inc.* Retrieved on September 18, 2016 from https://commonsenseenterprises.net/wp-content/uploads/2015/11/Succession-Planning-and-the-Emerging-Generations.pdf.

6. Smith, A. (2015, April 1). U.S. Smartphone Use in 2015. Chapter One: A Portrait of Smartphone Ownership. *Pew Research Center*. Retrieved on September 18, 2016 from www.pewinternet.org/2015/04/01/chapter-one-a-portrait-of-smartphone-ownership/.

7. Ibid.

8. Smith, A. (2015, April 1). U.S. Smartphone Use in 2015. Chapter Two: Usage and Attitudes toward Smartphones. *Pew Research Center*. Retrieved on September 18, 2016 from www.pewinternet.org/2015/04/01/chapter-two-usage-and-attitudes-toward-smartphones/.

9. Ibid.

10. Wendover, B. (2009, December 4). *The Next Generation.* Retrieved on September 18, 2016 from https://commonsenseenterprises.net/the-next-generation-what-will-the-generation-after-the-millennials-generation-y-be-called-what-do-you-know-about-their-values-and-expectations/.

11. Ibid.

12. Lenhart, A. (2010, September 2). Cell Phones and American Adults. *Pew Research Center*. Retrieved on September 18, 2016 from www.pewinternet.org/2010/09/02/cell-phones-and-american-adults/.

13. Speak Up. (2015). *Research Project Findings: Ten Things Everyone Should Know About K-12 Students' Digital Learning.* Retrieved on September 18, 2016 from www.tomorrow.org/speakup/pdfs/10-things-students-speak-up-2015-national.pdf.

14. Ibid.

15. Project Tomorrow. (2014). *The New Digital Learning Playbook, Advancing College and Career Ready Skills Development in K–12 Schools.* Retrieved on September 18, 2016 from www.tomorrow.org/speakup/SU13DigitalLearningPlaybook_EducatorReport.html.

16. *YouTube Press Statistics.* Retrieved on September 16, 2016 from www.youtube.com/yt/press/statistics.html.

17. Hirshberg. (2009, December 11). *Howard Rheingold on Technology and Education* [video file]. Retrieved from http://youtube/bI6Q_1V7XJ8.

18. To download the list of references for this particular "Brain Rule," visit www.brainrules.net/pdf/references_multisensory.pdf.

19. To download list of references for this particular "Brain Rule," visit www.brainrules.net/pdf/references_vision.pdf.

Chapter 1

Building a Solid Foundation

The first semester I integrated a social network into my online art appreciation class, I had a student come to me with an unexpected concern. That concern was an important moment for me, as it made me think more carefully about how my use of new technologies affected each student in different ways.

The semester was in its first few days, and most of the students had already joined our network and were enthusiastically sharing photographs on their personal page—ranging from family vacation photos taken at the Louvre to pictures of their families and pets. I excitedly lurked in the network and enjoyed reading the student-student dialogue that was prompted by the photographs: "Hey, I went there on a family vacation too. When were you there?" Or, "Your dog is adorable. He looks like a dog I used to have." Or, my favorite, "I remember you! You were in my geography class last semester!" I think about these early personal communications in an online class as being the early whispers of community building—kind of like the chatter and pre-class conversation that occurs in a hallway or in a classroom before the instructor begins speaking.

However, the student who came to me with a concern wasn't so keen on the idea of interacting with her peers in our social network. In fact, she sent me a thoughtful email explaining that she "isn't a teen-ager" and doesn't have any interest in being part of a class that resembles something like Myspace (this story took place pre-Facebook). That email changed my understanding of what it means to teach effectively with emerging technologies. It made me think more inclusively about who my students are and how their own experiences contribute to the way they learn. While my younger students generally jumped into the social network enthusiastically, my older students weren't yet engaged in social networking and were suspicious and unsure about how it could correlate with a college class.

It was important for me to take this concern seriously. First, I was pleased that she felt comfortable enough to bring it to my attention and realized there were probably other students who might be compelled to drop a class rather than engage their instructor in a discussion about the learning environment. Second, I realized that her reluctance was an effect of me being ineffective in how I contextualized the technology into my class and introduced my expectations to my students. This chapter provides strategies that will help ameliorate student concerns like the one I've shared here.

Supporting Student Success

For a moment, shift your viewpoint and think about your class(es) from the perspective of your students. Most students register for classes to fulfill requirements and know very little about the actual class (expectations, requirements, etc.) until the class begins—that is, perhaps other than what they read on RateMyProfessors.com. Really, what happens when a student begins a class is she enters a learning environment. The first time she engages with that environment, she begins to understand what is expected of her, what the experience will be like, and what her role in the process will be. And, more than likely, she is simultaneously registered for several other "environments" that will each be distinct. It's up to her to navigate these environments successfully, and this can be a tricky—even daunting—task.

Now imagine being that student and having each of those learning environments shift *unexpectedly* throughout their duration. Unexpected shifts in a class are like unexpected turbulence on an airplane. They are uncomfortable and stressful. Teaching with emerging technologies can be like flying with unexpected turbulence if they aren't integrated into a learning environment effectively.

While today's traditional college-age students are more comfortable with experimenting with new technologies than previous generations, they aren't necessarily fluent in all tools, nor do they understand how to use them to be productive lifelong learners, which, I believe, is a skill that all college classes can contribute to developing. Moreover, college classes can consist of generationally diverse groups of students. You'll have students, much like my apprehensive student, who become anxious at the prospect of taking a class that integrates technologies they've never used. The key to supporting the success of *all* your students is to start students off on a solid foot the moment a class begins. Implementing the strategies outlined in this chapter will ensure your students are clear, from the start, about *why* you are requiring them to use tools in your class, *how* the tools will enhance their experiences, and what is appropriate and inappropriate behavior and content.

As you integrate emerging technologies into your classes, strive to communicate the following items in your course syllabus and share them with your students on or before the first day of class:

List of Tools That Will Be Used and Your Reason(s) for Using Each

Upon entering a class, students should have an opportunity to preview the supplemental tools you plan to have them use. This does not imply that you cannot use a tool not shared on the list; it's merely an effort to communicate your plans to students so they have a clear picture of the road ahead.

As noted earlier, sharing this information with students *before* the start of a class, even before they register for a class, is ideal, as it empowers students to be able to register for classes that meet their own learning styles and overall preferences. Today, we have many students who are enthusiastic about using mobile apps or social media in a class, but, at the same time, we also have multiple generations of students on college campuses now, students with disabilities that may be challenged by using particular tools, and others that may be supported more effectively in a rich-media environment. Considering the student experience is an essential part of teaching effectively with emerging technologies.

With that said, students also want to understand *why* you are using the technologies. This is important to share for two reasons. First, because it illuminates the connection between learning (the student's goal) and technology. Sadly, only about half of college students feel that their professors use technology effectively.[1] So don't expect your students to feel excited about using a new tool or two until you can lucidly demonstrate why it's relevant to their success. Second, hearing your explanation may turn a reluctant baby boomer with little to no technology skills into a curious learner who is ready to try something new. Moreover, this can be an empowering experience for both the student and the instructor.

Here is a sample I've written:

> *In this class, you will create your own blog using WordPress, a free blogging platform. Alternatively, if you would prefer to use a different blogging tool, just*

let me know. A blog is a website that is similar to an online journal. You will regularly add new entries or "posts" to your blog that will reflect on your learning in this class.

Creating your own blog will provide you with your very own website to examine, analyze, and discuss the content you will engage with in this class. You will find that blogging is quite different from writing a paper and submitting it to your professor for a grade. Your blog will be shared with your peers and the rest of the world, placing your unique ideas and perspectives in a collective, living, and global dialogue about our topics.

Your blog will extend you the opportunity to connect with people around the world who are engaging with similar topics, to receive comments from these individuals, and to inspire ideas for other bloggers. At the end of our class, you will have a living product that will remain active beyond the end of this term.

List of Required Supplemental Equipment

What equipment do students need to possess (or have access to) for your class? Most colleges and universities have basic technology requirements that are communicated to online students prior to registration (computer, browser, high-speed Internet connection). If you are teaching a face-to-face or hybrid class with emerging technologies, it's critical to establish a similar toolkit—this may be something already established and shared on your campus, or it may be up to you to get this conversation initiated.

In addition to the tools and equipment needed to access your class, however, you must also clearly communicate the equipment students will need to contribute to your class. In your list, it may be more appropriate to encourage students to "have access" to the tools rather than require them to be purchased.

Supplemental equipment for learning may include the following:

- webcam* (for participating in a video web conference or recording video presentations)
- microphone* (for having online voice conversations during office hours, recording an audio presentation, leaving a voice comment in a discussion, interviewing an artist in Mexico, recording a variety of opinions about a current event)

- smartphone or other device that can take digital pictures (to document a field trip, identify a biological specimen, share examples of local architecture that demonstrate influence from ancient civilizations)

Access Expectations and Resources

Campus Access

Is the equipment available for student use on campus? You may need to do some research in this area. Visit your campus computer labs or reach out and contact the appropriate campus representatives. If the answer is "no," it's important for you to share the need for these resources with your colleagues involved with planning efforts. Today's typical college or university provides students with access to Wi-Fi and computers, but some provide private audio- and video-recording stations, as well as mobile lounges in which students can check out mobile tablets for completing course assignments. Also, keep in mind that some campuses still block the use of some social media sites in computer labs. If you are having your students interact in a Facebook group, view or share videos on YouTube, or engage in a chat on Twitter, then you should identify if your students have access to these sites from computer labs on campus.

Discounts or Special Pricing

Are the tools you are encouraging your students to use available in your campus bookstore or through an online partner at a discounted rate? For example, the Foundation for California Community Colleges has developed "College Buys," an online portal that provides discounts on software and hardware to students, faculty, and campuses. If you are aware of resources like this, be sure to share them with your students (and your peers!)

Necessary Software

Will your students need to download and install or use any applications to complete class assignments and projects? Providing this information to students ahead of time will allow them to make alternative access plans. Also, it's a good idea to encourage students to upgrade to the most recent version of the applications on your list (including web browsers). Include a direct link to the website(s) when possible.

Supplemental Mobile Apps

Chances are most of the students in your classes have a smartphone. According to the Pew Research Center, 92% of Americans age 18–34 own a smartphone.[2] Compiling a list of mobile apps that students could use to support their learning in your class is a great idea. Keep your eyes peeled for the "mobile" icon throughout this book to identify emerging technologies that may be used with mobile devices, but also take some time to peruse the apps available that align with your own discipline. You may be surprised at the great resources you discover!

Examples

You will have many students who are not familiar with the technologies you've identified, so it's always a great idea to include a link to an example of a podcast, a wiki project, a collaborative mind map, etc. Seeing an actual example will relieve a student's anxiety and help him or her understand what to expect more clearly. You may also consider including screenshots of the environments in your syllabus.

 TIP!

Use Jing for Easy Screenshots and Screencasts

There are many ways to create screenshots (still images of your computer screen) and screencasts (videos of your computer screen). My favorite free tool is Jing. It runs on both PCs and Macs, and produces .png files that can easily be annotated and saved to your computer, as well as screencasts that can be shared online via a free Screencast. com account or downloaded and then shared within a course management system or website. See Chapter 4 for further discussion.

Student Perspectives

It's amazing how much more relevant advice is to a student when the advice comes from another student rather than a professor. Our society has swiftly evolved into a participatory culture, placing peer reviews at our fingertips before we dine at a restaurant, vacation at a hotel, or buy a book. Students want to hear from other students about what they should expect in a class—and that desire is the fuel behind the popularity of RateMyProfessors.com.

SHOWCASE

Wisdom Wall

Figure 1.1
Screenshot of wisdom wall.

Here is a creative, fun, and easy way to use a collaborative tool such as Google Docs, Voice-Thread, or Flipgrid to share past student perspectives with incoming students and start to build community in your class. Provide students with a link to the *Wisdom Wall* at the beginning of a new class. The Wisdom Wall is a collection of advice contributed by students from the previous term.

The advice the students share with each other consistently impresses me, and, honestly, I learn a great deal from the comments myself!

Sample Wisdom Wall Contributions

"It may seem like a lot of work at first but just breathe and try not to get overwhelmed as this class is very rewarding. Just be sure that you keep up with your blog posts ... and do your VoiceThreads and you will do great!"

"Don't be afraid of all the technology. The teacher is really good about showing you step-by-step how to do everything and after a while it gets easy and starts to become fun."

"If you are dreading this class, listen up! Michelle makes this class so interesting and exciting. You will be learning and enjoying the class before you can say yuck ... This class was awesome!"

"The main advice I can give is DO NOT GET BEHIND ... If you choose to procrastinate you will not be happy with the results because things pile up quickly and unexpectedly."

How to Create a Wisdom Wall

Coordinating the Wisdom Wall can be a very simple process or it can be a time-consuming task. One option would be to have students email their "advice" to you and then you'd be responsible for curating a display of the feedback on a website or in your course management system. At the end and beginning of a new term, there are many other, more important, tasks for you to focus on. So empower your students to be able to create the Wisdom Wall on their own!

Here's an easy solution: Create a Google Doc (see Chapter 5 for more information). Adjust the share settings so the doc can be edited by anyone with the link. Then include the link to the doc in your course. In essence, selecting the following settings transforms a Google Doc into a wiki page:

1.   Refer to the online Google Drive Help Center for instructions to change your share settings in Google Drive: https://support.google.com/drive
2.   At the top of your doc, compose clear instructions to students. I prefer to say, "Click in the white space below the red horizontal line and type your advice to my future students." Then insert a simple horizontal red line below the instructions.
3.   If you prefer, create a fun graphic and insert it at the top of your Wisdom Wall. I created the graffiti text in Figure 1.1 using the Graffiti Creator (GraffitiCreator.net/), took a screenshot of it, saved it to my computer, and then uploaded it into my Google Doc.
4.   Paste the link to the Wisdom Wall Google Doc in your course management system and encourage your students to leave their advice by a particular time and date.

Building Community

The mainstream use of social technologies such as Facebook, YouTube, Twitter, and Instagram has transformed learning outside the college classroom into a rich community-based experience. Each year, more and more traditional college-age students enter our classrooms with an intimate understanding of the relevance and value that participatory learning provides. As Cathy Davidson and David Goldberg noted in *The Future of Thinking*:

> Since the current generation of college students has no memory of the historical moment before the advent of the Internet, we are suggesting that participatory learning as a practice is no longer exotic or new but a commonplace way of socializing and learning. For many, it seems entirely unremarkable.[3]

Participatory learning simply "looks" different from traditional college learning. In most college classrooms, learning has historically relied upon the successful transfer of information from a subject-matter expert (professor) to a receptacle (student). This traditional model expects students to play a passive role in learning. In contrast, participatory learning situates individuals within a fluid community in which members make contributions by sharing ideas of their own and responses to the contributions made by other members. Other community members comment on those contributions, leading to further dialogue, refinement, growth, and debate. The intermeshing of community members in a participatory learning environment is grounded in clear "community guidelines" that are a stipulation of joining the community.

Figure 1.2 Video still, "My Space in the Room" by Derek Schneweis. Used with permission.

Michael Wesch's 2011 video, "'The Visions of Students Today' 2011 Remix One," is a compilation of student-generated videos submitted in response to Wesch's call. The video conveys experiences of 21st-century college "learners" who are immersed in traditional lecture classes and wondering what their peers are thinking and feeling. The student contributions suggest that they perceive their opinions and thoughts to be irrelevant in the classroom. The students convey a sense of feeling excluded from the process of constructing knowledge and understanding. To me, the video (a still from which is shown in Figure 1.2) illustrates the relevance gap between our mainstream teaching pedagogy and the effects of our students' participatory learning experiences outside the walls of college.[4]

Integrating emerging technologies into your college classroom does not necessarily mean you will transform your class into a participatory learning community. However, it does extend this opportunity to you, and it's a concept that you should think about as you begin to experiment and understand the technologies you will employ. For those professors who wish to create a community-based learning experience for students, it's necessary to realize that you will need to explicitly frame your class in this way from the very first day of class and then cultivate a learning environment that fosters and encourages trust, student contributions, peer comments, and the overall collaborative construction of knowledge. This vision of learning should inform the decisions you make about tools to use in your class.

Class Philosophy

Compose a brief description of the type of learning environment your students should expect and include this in your syllabus. Each college professor has his/her own style. Communicating how you approach your class and the role that emerging technologies play will allow you to share your style and expectations, and encourage students to be more productive. However, the most important element of a class philosophy is making a commitment to modeling it throughout the semester. A philosophy is only words on a page—the time your students spend in your class will infuse it with meaning.

Sample Online Class Philosophy (CC-BY Michelle Pacansky-Brock)

This class is a community. We all have the same objective: to learn. Online students often feel isolated, but it's important to know you are not in this alone! I need each of you to approach our online class with a great attitude and a willingness to help each other. Many problems and questions can be resolved by asking a fellow student. I am always here to help you, but I truly believe your experience will be better if you communicate with your fellow students throughout the semester. The technologies woven into this class will increase your ability to share, connect, and learn from one another.

Sample Face-to-Face Class Philosophy (CC-BY Michelle Pacansky-Brock)

This is not a typical "lecture" class. In "lecture" classes, students come to class and passively receive information delivered via lecture format. Throughout the semester, you will be completing regular web-based assignments prior to coming to class. This will include micro lectures, videos, and readings that may be accessed on a computer or smartphone. Rather than using class time passively, you will actively participate in critical analysis, discussion, and debate as we apply the ideas from the digital course materials. Your full commitment to the format of this class is critical to your success.

Every person in this class is part of a community focused on learning. Throughout the semester, you will be expected to help each other, and you will learn to rely upon each other. You will treat each other with respect and should always feel comfortable approaching one another for help. I will do everything in my power to create a trustworthy, stimulating, active learning experience for you. As your instructor, I am here to facilitate your learning and guide you each step of the way. I am also here for you to discuss any problems or challenges you are having. Please don't ever hesitate to contact me via email or phone or visit me during office hours.

My role is dependent upon having a group of individuals who are committed to being here for every class and being ready to contribute keen insights and perspectives to our discussions. We are in this together! This class will not be a success if you do not hold up your end of the bargain. Deal?

Community Groundrules

Communities thrive through the active contributions of their members. Students need to feel safe and perceive their learning environment as a trusted space to share and collaborate with their peers. Developing a clear set of community groundrules and sharing them with your students is imperative. Aside from developing the set of rules, it's critical that you weave them into the use of the participatory tools you'll be using. Agreeing to the groundrules could be made a condition of participation, for example, and/or you could share your groundrules on a website (a simple Google Doc will do for those of you without knowledge of html or a process for hosting your content) and link to it from the assignments you share in your course management system. Essentially, keeping the groundrules at the surface of your students' participation is important, as this approach serves to remind them of their expectations and also provides an opportunity for you to communicate how students should deal with violations. The groundrules empower students to play a central, rather than peripheral, role in their learning.

Sample Community Groundrules (CC-BY Michelle Pacansky-Brock)

A community is a group of individuals who work together to support a common goal or interest. We are working together to support the successful achievement of our learning outcomes. In an effort to ensure our community develops, thrives, and sustains throughout our time together, the following groundrules will be in effect at all times.

- Treat contributions made by other members of the class with respect.
- Reach out and help when you see the need. And ask for help when you need it.
- Back up your contributions. As with any content you share online, keeping an alternative copy is essential. Each community member is responsible for keeping a backup of his/her contributions.
- Have patience and a sense of humor with technology. There will be hiccups, expect them.
- Keep an open mind. If you're feeling reluctant, that's OK. Take it one step at a time and look at this as an opportunity to learn something new.
- Contribute regularly to collaborative activities to ensure other members of the community have ample opportunity to read/listen, reflect, and respond to your ideas.

- Respect the diverse opinions and viewpoints of each member of our community. Differences allow us to learn and grow together.
- Understand that communications shared through text have a higher likelihood of being misinterpreted than the spoken word. Therefore, when you type a thought or a comment, read it carefully before you submit it. If you question the way it is worded, read it out loud to yourself. If you still question the way it's phrased, rewrite it.
- Contribute regularly to group dialogue, including blog posts and replies. The contributions of each individual play a role in the collective strength and diversity of our community.
- Members of our community are to be restricted to enrolled members of our class in an effort to maintain a safe, trustworthy discussion environment.
- All image and video content shared within this community will reflect acceptable content standards. You are expected to use discretion and, if asked, you will be expected to demonstrate how your content supports the theme of our community: "[enter a description of the community's theme here]."
- Understand that any network member has the ability to create a new forum in our network. However, s/he who creates the forum immediately takes on the responsibility of moderating it. This means you have committed to regularly responding to new comments and greeting new members of the forum or group.
- If, at any time, you feel that any of these groundrules have been violated by a member of our community, you are encouraged to bring your concern directly and immediately to [enter professor name], our community leader. Clearly identify which groundrule has been violated and include specific evidence of the violation in your email. Your concerns will be addressed promptly with careful consideration in an individualized manner.
- After this class is over, your access to this community will end. If you share content that you'd like to preserve, it is your responsibility to make a backup of it before the class ends.

 **TIP!**

Write a general set of community groundrules that apply to all of your classes. Type them up into a Google Doc and include the link in each syllabus/course.

Empower Students to Prepare Prior to the Start of Class

Emerging technologies provide many options for professors and institutions to increase a student's readiness for the start of a new term. Our newly participatory society has crafted higher expectations for understanding precisely what an experience will be like before it begins or before a purchase is made. When I visit Amazon. com to purchase a book, for example, I read the reviews left by other users before I make my decision. When my 14-year-old son wants to purchase a new video game, he goes online and reads the reviews left by other users to decide whether or not it's worth his money, or if the advertisements are just a slick persuasive tactic. When I'm traveling, I'll pull out my smartphone and check the reviews of a restaurant on Yelp before I decide to dine there. Our participatory society has empowered us as consumers to be informed and to make choices that are tailored to our preferences, needs, and expectations before we make a decision to take the plunge.

Unfortunately, things don't work this way in the world of higher education. But I like to imagine how different things would be if they did. Now we can easily make the argument that students *want* to know about their professors and the expectations that will be placed upon them after registering for a course. This desire is easily confirmed by considering the wild popularity of RateMyProfessors.com. At the time of writing this, the site boasts that it shares more than 15 million student-generated ratings of over 1.4 million professors (up about 50% from the first edition of this book!). And the site is viewed by more than four million college students each month.[5]

Trying to gain insight about a professor or a particular class is part of the age-old student experience. I know I made efforts to gain insight about my professors before registering for a class when I was in college, and I bet you did too. But, imagine with me, if students had the opportunity to learn about you directly from *you*, rather than tap into what other students thought about you. Why don't we share our syllabi online for students to review prior to registering for a class? Why don't we record a video introduction and share it online so students can get a sense of who we are, the person they'll be spending 50 hours with over the course of a semester?

The Web 2.0 era has empowered each of us to become content creators. We can now easily record video direct from a webcam into a free YouTube account and embed it on a website. And we are no longer barred from creating a website because we don't know html or because we don't have server space. There are many options available to us now.

If you like the idea of sharing your course expectations, syllabus, and other critical resources with your students before they register for your class but don't have the resources to develop a traditional website, consider designing a "liquid syllabus" using a free micropublishing tool such as Adobe Spark Page or Populr.me (see Chapter 4 for details).

The Nuts 'n' Bolts of Teaching on the Web

The nuts 'n' bolts of how you integrate emerging technologies into your teaching will hinge partially on your existing technological infrastructure. What is the central access point for your students outside of your physical classroom? Most institutions these days provide professors teaching online, hybrid, or face-to-face classes with access to a learning management system or LMS (Canvas, Blackboard, Moodle, etc.), while other professors independently use eLearning resources provided through a publisher or have a simple website or blog on which they share links to resources and web-based activities.

A learning management system (which may also be referred to as a course management system or CMS) is proprietary or open source software that contains some basic functions: an area for announcements, storing content in a hierarchic structure, traditional assessments (quizzes, exams), a discussion board, and a grade book. Additional functions vary by LMS (and version) but may also include blogs, wikis, ePortfolios, and web-conferencing platforms.

LMSs are excellent tools for organizing content into a clear, consistent learning path for your students. They provide a centralized location for sharing pertinent course materials with students who are registered for your class. LMSs also require students to authenticate so you are ensured the students who access the material you share are enrolled in your class, and they also provide options for tracking student log-ins, access to content, and participation. Student authentication supports the construction of a safe, trustworthy learning environment, and the gradebook included with a LMS is an essential, secure portal for sharing private information with students.

However, many college instructors today are less than thrilled with the tools commonly included in the LMS toolkit for delivering awe-inspiring learning and, therefore, experiment with the wealth of web-based, social technologies that allow for easy content creation and sharing. This section will touch on three important elements to keep in mind as you integrate emerging technologies into your students' learning:

- embedding versus linking
- ensuring student privacy
- using copyrighted material for teaching

Embedding versus Linking

Frequently, teaching with emerging technologies involves the integration of content from another website into your online course. When you integrate that content, it's important to think carefully about how to integrate it most effectively to avoid derailing the flow of your students' learning. Embedding content into your online class is like taking a pair of scissors, cutting the content out from the secondary web page, and gluing it onto a page in your LMS, eLearning portal, or website. Linking to content, essentially, appears as an active URL or hyperlinked text on a page. Clicking on the URL link or hyperlinked text opens a new window or tab, displaying an external web page to view and interact with the content you've shared with them.

Embedding content from other websites is an effective way to keep your students focused on the content inside your main access portal rather than fragmenting their experience by going out to multiple websites. You may find it helpful to realize that many students who are sent out to another website get sidetracked and don't come back to the class. (Can you relate? I know I can!) Identify whether or not embedding the content in your primary content portal is an option. If it is, is the embedded version effective or is it best to provide both the embedded and linked version? Here are some things to keep in mind.

Is Embedding an Option?

Most web-based tools provide the option to embed content elsewhere, but it's important to be sure. To check, look for a "Share" or "Publish" option within the tool you are using; this is typically where you'll find the "embed" option, if it exists. If you see an embed option, the site will provide a string of "embed code," which is a snippet of code that a browser interprets and, in turn, displays a "cutout" of your web-based content. The code you copy will specify the dimensions of the embedded object. Some sites provide different size options or allow you to customize the embed code. When selecting a particular size, you'll want to be sure it fits within the display area of your course (this is a process of trial and error). When you locate the embed code, highlight the entire string of code and copy it to your computer's clipboard. (To copy on a PC, press Control + C. To copy on a Mac, press Command + C.)

Locate the Visual Text Box Editor

You can easily embed content in an LMS, an eLearning portal, or a web page. The key is locating the visual text box editor. Many experienced LMS users are

Figure 1.3 Screenshot of visual text box editor 1.

Image provided with permission of Instructure, Inc. © Instructure, Inc.

not aware of this option. The visual text box editor is a function within an LMS that is usually made available to users by default, but I have seen some instances in which institutions disable this feature. Visual text box editors will vary in appearance, but they should look something like the one shown in Figure 1.3.

Provide Supplementary Information about the Content

Before you paste your embed code in the visual text box editor, it may be a good idea to introduce the content you are embedding (if you haven't already done this somewhere else). If it's a video you are embedding, type a simple description in the text box that introduces its topic and tells students how long it is. If it's a video without captions, you may provide a link to a transcript for students who require this accommodation (Figure 1.4).

Toggle to HTML Source Code View

This is a critical step. Before you paste the embed code into the text box, you must switch from rich text mode (which shows text the way it will appear to your students) to html source code view. How to do this varies, but usually the action is performed by clicking on a button that looks like this "< >," or you may see a button or tab that says "HTML." Click on the appropriate icon and then paste the code into the blank space below the existing text (see Figure 1.5).

Save

Click the necessary buttons (save, continue, etc.), and you should now see your embedded object below the supplementary information (see Figure 1.6).

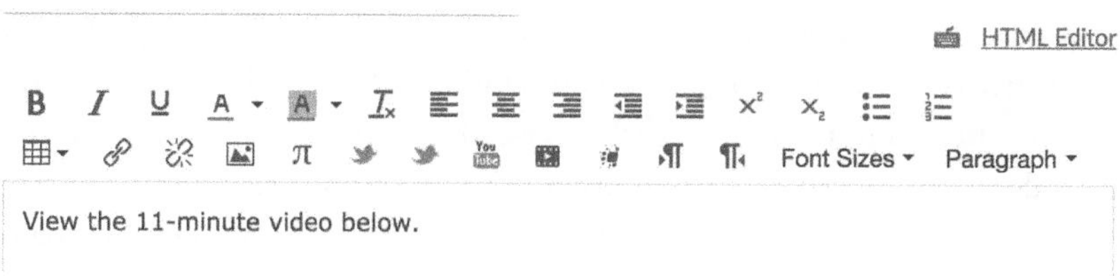

HTML Editor

B *I* U A ▾ A ▾ I_x ≡ ≡ ≡ ≡ ≡ x² x₂ ≔ ≔
⊞▾ 🔗 🔗 🖼 π 🐦 🐦 ▶ ▣ ♯ ¶ ¶◀ Font Sizes ▾ Paragraph ▾

View the 11-minute video below.

Figure 1.4 Screenshot of visual text box editor 2.

Image provided with permission of Instructure, Inc. © Instructure, Inc.

Rich Content Editor

```
<p>View the 11-minute video below.</p>
<p> </p>
<iframe src="https://player.vimeo.com/video/2853950" width="640" height="427" frameborder="0"
webkitallowfullscreen mozallowfullscreen allowfullscreen></iframe>
<p><a href="https://vimeo.com/2853950">Chalk to iPod: 21st Century Higher Education, Generational
Challenges and Opportunities</a> from <a href="https://vimeo.com/brocansky">Michelle Pacansky-
Brock</a> on <a href="https://vimeo.com">Vimeo</a>.</p>
```

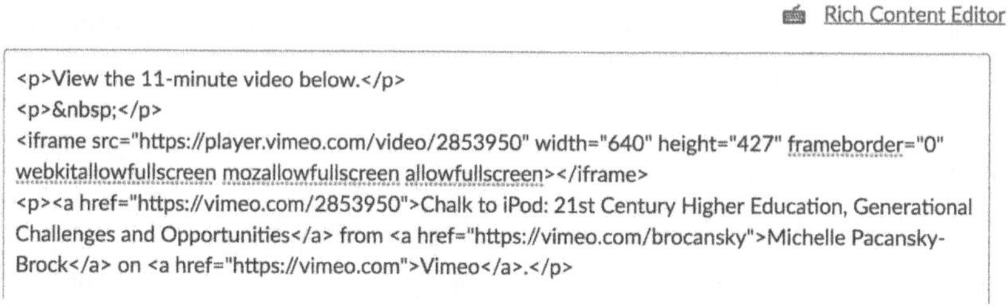

Figure 1.5 Screenshot of visual text box editor with embed code.

Image provided with permission of Instructure, Inc. © Instructure, Inc.

View the 11-minute video below.

Figure 1.6 Screenshot of embedded video.

Student Privacy

For centuries, college learning has occurred in a physical space partitioned from the rest of the world by four walls. The idea of encouraging or requiring students to interact with each other and share their work in digital format in the public web challenges the traditional paradigm of college learning in many ways. And frequently this change ushers in some alarming concerns about student privacy. Being concerned about the privacy of your students is certainly important but what's more important, possibly, is that we, as educators, provide opportunities for our students to learn how to responsibly participate in the online environment and mindfully re-use digital content. These are critical 21st-century skills that much of the population does not yet possess. Using emerging technologies in your college classroom is an opportunity to foster these relevant skills. Teaching effectively with emerging technologies requires you to facilitate meaningful, safe interactions in support of your students learning—which is nothing new. How to achieve this objective with emerging technologies is new. Here are some things to consider.

Identify the Tool-Specific Privacy Settings

As you evaluate tools for adoption in your teaching (which is the focus of Chapter 2), you'll want to spend time exploring the privacy options that are provided. Many tools will extend the option to share the content in different ways that may range from public display on the open web, retrievable through a web search, to private and requiring sign-on or a password, and anywhere in between. For example, I use a web-based tool called VoiceThread to foster participatory learning activities designed around images (for more information, reference the introduction, as well as Chapters 4 and 5). When I create a VoiceThread, it begins as a completely secure environment. For example, if I were to send the link to anyone else, that person could click on it but only see a message indicating that he/she doesn't have privileges to view it. I can easily make adjustments to this default setting by allowing "anyone" to view it (which actually means "anyone with the link," but it won't be found through a web search), or I could choose to have it included on VoiceThread's "Browse" page, making it fully public and retrievable through a web search. Similarly, if I share a video on YouTube, I have the option to mark the video "Public" (for anyone to find and view), "Unlisted" (which means it will not be found through a web search and will not appear in searches in YouTube but will be viewable by anyone who has access to the link), or "Private" (which requires me to type in the email addresses of the individuals who have my permission to view the video. This option requires the permitted users to sign in before viewing the video).

Select the Best Security Setting

The "best" security setting is not always the most secure. You need to think carefully about the environment you wish to cultivate with the content and manage your workload effectively. If you select the most secure option, you are going to be entering many emails (possibly hundreds, depending on how many students you have and how much teaching support you are provided) and, undoubtedly, dealing with many students who encounter log-in challenges. Frequently, the mid-range option is a great option, particularly if you are teaching in a LMS. If you copy the link to your content and share it within your LMS, then students must first authenticate to view and interact with the content. This doesn't make it impossible for the content to be shared outside of class, but it does reduce the likelihood of this occurring and eliminates the concern of having others find the content within a web search and leave comments that may be disruptive, inappropriate, or symptomatic of spam. With that said, one of your objectives may be to have your students participate in a global conversation about a particular topic. Perhaps you want your students to be able to invite others to contribute to the course dialogue, or you want them to have the opportunity to experience receiving commentary from the global community. If this is the case, then you may want to consider a fully public option and encourage your students to become effective monitors of spam and foster the ability to ferret out inappropriate contributors (both essential 21st-century skills.)

Inform Students about Who Their Audience Will Be

Don't expect students to understand intuitively who will have access to the content they contribute for your class. Be sure to explain this to students prior to their participation. If you are having students participate in public web-based activities, it's a very good idea to encourage them to sort through information that is appropriate to share. A good rule of thumb is to encourage students to abstain from sharing personal information about themselves and focus on fulfilling the course-related prompts and assignments.

Develop a Student Use Agreement

Develop and share a student use agreement in your syllabus and have students verify their acceptance through a written contract or by completing an automated "syllabus quiz" in your LMS in which they "accept" the agreement. This practice clearly informs students about the parameters of the environment you have constructed and also provides you with tangible verification of their acceptance of the parameters, thus providing practical protection for both you and your students.

Offer Options

Be prepared to offer students options about how students will represent themselves online. Here are some suggestions to consider. Encourage students to use their first name and last initial when sharing contributions. Be creative with avatars. Some students may not feel comfortable sharing a photograph of themselves. Encourage them to share an icon or image of something that represents who they are.

Provide Accommodations When Necessary

Be aware that there may be students who have valid privacy concerns about sharing contributions online. For example, I once had a student who was taking online classes because she had a restraining order against her husband and was afraid to leave her house. It's important that you create an environment in which students, first, have an opportunity to share these concerns with you and, second, have alternative options that allow them to contribute and learn along with the rest of the class in a safe, trustworthy environment. One strategy is to allow the option to use a pseudonym, with your approval, to preserve the anonymity of these students. But keep in mind that pseudonyms can complicate the assessment process, as you will need to identify the author of the anonymous content.

Do Not Share Grades

Student grades should always be kept private and shared in a secure environment that requires a user authentication, like a CMS. Email is not considered secure.

 **TIP!**

Download these Student Privacy Tips in a handy PDF from the Chapter 1 resources shared online at TeachingWithEmergingTech.com

---

Re-using Copyrighted Material for Teaching and Learning

Copyright is one of the most complex and dizzying topics in academia today. Our digital culture has flipped the logic of copyright on its head and, as a result, copyright restrictions are becoming increasingly more stringent, and teaching with digital materials is becoming more bewildering. Questions about the legality of using copyrighted material in your classes (in analog or digital form) should be brought to your respective campus representative(s). Individual colleges and institutions should have their own individual copyright policy to assist with guiding faculty through these muddy waters and protecting their own interests. The information provided here is offered for educational purposes and is not intended to replace the advice of your campus representatives or to serve as legal advice.

Understanding copyright in its historical context is a good place to start our conversation. In 1787, the writers of the U.S. Constitution included a clause in Article 1, Section 8 (arguably a sign of its significance) that has shaped the copyright laws we live with today.[6] The clause was guided by the interest to preserve the public's right to access knowledge without being limited by a creator's right to restrict access: "The Congress shall have Power To [. . .] promote the Progress of Science and Useful Arts, by securing for limited Times to Authors and Inventors the exclusive Right to their respective Writings and Discoveries."[7]

It may seem contradictory to understand that copyright law exists to *promote* public access to knowledge when, from my experiences, many professors today live in fear of being slapped with a lawsuit for violating copyright law. For the owner of the copyright has the exclusive right to govern who may use the work only after receiving express written authorization from the copyright owner to do so. This fear often prevents educators from sharing content that contains copyrighted works, even when their distribution of the materials may fall well within fair use (see the description in the next section). When copyright of a work expires, the work enters the public domain and may be used, at that time, without authorization. However, understanding when a work enters the public domain isn't so easy (and varies by country).[8]

Fair Use

The fair use clause of copyright (section 107) further supports the interest of promoting public access to knowledge by permitting the use of copyrighted material without the permission of the copyright owner for certain purposes (including teaching, scholarship, and research). However, to determine whether a particular use of a copyrighted work is fair, four factors must be considered.

- The purpose and character of the use, including whether such use is of a commercial nature or is for non-profit educational purposes.
- The nature of the copyrighted work.

- The amount and substantiality of the portion used in relation to the copyrighted work as a whole.
- The effect of the use upon the potential market for or value of the copyrighted work.

(Title 17, Section 107 United States Code)

So, with this information clearly spelled out, it should be simple to identify whether or not a particular use of a copyrighted work for teaching, scholarship, or research falls into fair use, right? Well, it's not. And digital content makes this process more ambiguous, as the definition of a "copy" is no longer clear-cut. In fact, you will never be able to ascertain a hard "yes" or "no" to whether or not a use is fair. What's critical is that you understand the four factors of fair use and are able to apply them with good judgment in your own teaching, following your institutional guidelines (which, for example, may provide a more clear definition of what your college/university has determined to be "the amount and substantiality of the portion used"). There are also some very helpful tools that have been developed to assist with this process. If a copyright owner feels that you have overstepped the boundaries of fair use, there may be the need to address how the use of work applies to each of the four factors.

Open Licenses

Creativity in the 21st century is deeply informed through remixing, which involves a process of using existing material to create something new. Remixing, a product of our digital society, deeply informs contemporary creative expression, and you'll find examples of it on YouTube, Flickr, Twitter, Instagram, and other social media outlets. In remix culture, "fair use is your friend," as the Center for Social Media has so eloquently argued in its clear and informative video shared about video remixing.[9]

But as videos are now recorded daily with mobile phones and other devices and shared via social media tools and unattributed photographic images are downloaded and redistributed on other websites, it becomes increasingly difficult to ensure the content one shares does not include copyrighted material. For example, if I were to take out my phone and record my niece jumping for a balloon and I happen to record a popular song playing in the background, I would violate copyright law. Now that's probably not going to be an issue if I keep that video between my family and me. However, when I click the "Share to YouTube" button on my phone and publicly share it with the world, that's a different story. No, I didn't intentionally use copyrighted material without the permission of the copyright owner, nonetheless, I did, and that's a violation of the law. Why is this really such a big deal? Well, imagine if I were a documentary filmmaker who captured a copyrighted song in the background of a key interview. I could be required to pay thousands of dollars in royalty fees for the licensing rights to use that song—which would directly undercut my creativity as well as the progress of filmmaking in general.[10]

While instances like these continue to wreak havoc on the logic of copyright law and the tenuous balance between the rights of authors/creators and public access to knowledge, there is some relief. Thanks to some creative and progressive thinkers, there are now several license options that copyright owners may choose to apply to their original works (without releasing their rights under traditional copyright law). These new flexible options are referred to as "open" licenses. When a copyright owner applies an open license to his work, it clearly specifies how and under what circumstances another person may re-use the work *without permission*. As public knowledge and understanding about open licenses continues to spread, more and more copyright owners are applying open licenses to their work and, in turn, there is an increasing supply of content that is easily accessible and may be redistributed and remixed without the anxiety of a looming lawsuit. Further, the energy stimulated through the use of open licensed content is fostering a culture of sharing that, arguably, in the 21st century promotes public access to knowledge more so than traditional copyright.

Creative Commons

One of the most popular open licenses today is Creative Commons (CC). Founded in 2001 with support from the Center for the Public Domain, CC has grown to support projects and licenses for works in more than 70 jurisdictions.[11] CC has become the "global standard for sharing across culture, education, government, science, and more."[12] To gain further clarity about how CC licenses work, it's helpful to think about them as a license option that falls somewhere between traditional copyright and the public domain, as illustrated in Figure 1.7. A work that is shared with a CC license clearly specifies how and under what circumstances a work may be used without the permission of the copyright owner. These conditions include one or more of the following: attribution (giving credit to the copyright owner), no derivatives (the work must be shared unchanged and in its entirety), share alike (new creations that use the work must be shared under an identical license), non-commercial (the work may not be used for commercial purposes).

Creators can easily discern which license is best for their work by using the Creative Commons *License Chooser*.[13] Licenses may be applied to digital works

Copyright	Creative Commons	Public Domain
All Rights Reserved	**Some Rights Reserved**	**No Rights Reserved**
Re-use requires permission from the copyright owner.	Use is allowed without permission *under the conditions noted in the license.*	Use is allowed without permission, as there is no copyright owner of a work in the public domain.

Figure 1.7 Permissible use of Creative Commons licensed works.

through the inclusion of an image of the license and websites containing digital works may embed a snippet of html code into the page, which allows for the content to be found and used more easily.

As educators utilizing emerging technologies for teaching and learning, understanding the value that sharing brings to our culture is critical. Learning, after all, doesn't occur without the sharing of knowledge. As you move forward with the creation of your own content in digital form, consider applying a CC license to your work and play a role in changing the world.

HOW TO FIND CREATIVE COMMONS–LICENSED WORKS

Creative Commons is largely based on community participation and works that utilize a CC license do not enter a database that can be accessed and searched directly. However, there is a portal page that will connect you with several useful content searches that will assist you with locating pertinent CC-licensed content. Keep in mind that it is your responsibility to ensure the content you find through a search on the following portal is, in fact, shared through a CC license.

1. Go to the Creative Commons Search portal at: Search.CreativeCommons. org.
2. Click on one of the options that aligns with the media type you are seeking: Flickr (image), YouTube (video), Jamendo (music), SpinXpress (media), etc.

 TIP!

Downloading Images from the Web Is Easy

If you are on a PC, right mouse click on the image and select the "Save Image As" option from the drop-down menu. If you are on a Mac (and don't have a right mouse click option), press "Control" and click on the image. Then select the "Save Image As" option from the drop-down menu and save the image file to your computer.

 TIP!

A Simple Way to Keep Track of Image License Details

I use Flickr a lot to find images for use in my digital work. I have found that it can be very easy to forget the name of the author and keep track of the license type of each image after I download them to my computer. I have found it useful to save the image with a filename that includes the author name and the details of the license. For example, a photograph of a yellow flower by John Catskill with an Attribution-No-Derivative-Non-Commercial license would be saved as, "Yellow Flower by John Catskill CC-BY-ND-NC.jpg"

 TIP!

Tools for Managing the Attribution of Images

Another way to manage the attribution of images you download from the web is to annotate the attribution on the image itself. This requires a tool that supports annotations. On my computer (I have a Mac), I regularly use Preview to do this. Alternatively, PicMonkey is a free, online tool that you can use to annotate images and then download them to your computer without creating an account. Avoid using screenshot tools for this purpose, however, as you are likely to reduce the quality of the digital image when taking a screenshot of it. Finally, some tools that utilize re-use of images are starting to incorporate the attributions during the creation process. For example, HaikuDeck and Adobe Spark, tools discussed in Chapter 4, and Photos for Class, a simple image search tool, offer this feature.

Learning from Student Frustrations

At the start of this chapter, I shared a story about a student who was reluctant to engage in the social network I had integrated into my class. After that student reached out to me, we engaged in a dialogue—I listened to her concerns and responded with more context, explaining why I had integrated the tool into the class, shared comments from previous students about how it had helped them stay connected and engaged, and encouraged her to keep an open mind. In our exchange, I made it clear to her that the *only* thing she was *required* to do in the network was become a member and write a weekly blog post in response to prompts I provided in the corresponding learning modules. That was key to her success. After she had more clarity about what she was required to do and what was optional (the sharing of pictures, for example), she felt more comfortable in the social, participatory environment I had planned for the student-student interactions.

It was clear to me that this was a high-risk student who may drop the class and, for that reason, I stayed in close contact with her throughout the first few weeks of class. By week three, she had turned the corner, and she began contributing some very compelling reflections in our weekly blog post assignments. And by the end of the class, she shared something priceless with me. She wrote me an email in which she thanked me for listening to her concerns and reflected on the class as a successful learning experience. But there was one more thing she shared that, to me, stands out as one of my most memorable teaching moments. She told me that, for the first time in her life, she felt connected to a culture from which she had previously felt excluded. My class gave her the opportunity to learn what a "social network" was and how a "blog" works—these were words that were meaningless to her before. Whereas before the class she felt marginalized from the technological landscape surrounding her—viewing it as a space for "teen-agers"—after the class, she felt included and welcomed. And here's the best part—she is a teacher who has begun using emerging tools in her own classes.

Notes

*   Think mobile! Suggest applications students can use on their smartphones to record/host video and audio. Smartphones and tablets are terrific for creating digital media content.

1. Smith, S. & Borreson Caruso, J., Introduction by Kim, J. (2010). *The ECAR Study of Undergraduate Students and Information Technology, 2010*. (Research Study). Boulder, CO: EDUCAUSE Center for Applied Research. Retrieved from www. educause. edu/ecar.

2. Poushter, J. (2016, February 22). Smartphone Ownership and Internet Usage Continues to Climb in Emerging Economies. *Pew Research Center*. Retrieved from www.pewglobal.org/2016/02/22/smartphone-ownership-and-internet-usage-continues-to-climb-in-emerging-economies/.

3. Davidson, C., Goldberg, D. T., & Jones, Z. M. (2009). *The Future of Thinking: Learning Institutions in a Digital Age*. From the John D. and Catherine T. MacArthur Foundation Reports on Digital Media and Learning. Cambridge, MA: MIT Press.

4. Wesch, M. [mwesch]. (2011, Jan 26). *The Visions of Students Today*. [video remix]. Retrieved from www.youtube.com/user/mwesch#p/u/0/-_XNG3Mndww.

5. *Wolfram Alpha* [website]. Retrieved on February 20, 2012 from www.wolframalpha. com/entities/web_domains/ratemyprofessors.com/98/2v/kh/.

6. Brigham Young University's "Copyright 101" offers an exceptionally concise and useful online module about copyright that includes self-assessments: http://lib. byu.edu/departs/copyright/tutorial/intro/page1.htm.

7. *The Constitution of the United States of America.* Retrieved from http://caselaw. lp.findlaw.com/data/constitution/articles.html.

8. Cornell has shared a helpful online table to assist with identifying when a work enters public domain: http://copyright.cornell.edu/resources/publicdomain.cfm.

9. Center for Social Media. (n.d.). *Remix Culture: Fair Use Is Your Friend* [video recording]. Retrieved from www.centerforsocialmedia.org/fair-use/videos/podcasts/ remixculture-fair-use-your-friend.

10. For a lighthearted portrayal of the trials and tribulations of a documentary film-maker navigating traditional copyright regulations, see Duke's Center for the Study of the Public Domain. *Tales from the Public Domain: BOUND BY LAW?* Retrieved from www.law.duke.edu/cspd/comics/.

11. *Creative Commons CC Affiliate Network wiki.* Retrieved on August 23, 2011 from http://wiki.creativecommons.org/CC_Affiliate_Network.

12. Creative Commons. (n.d.). *History.* Retrieved from https://creativecommons. org/about/history.

13. Creative Commons. (n.d.). *License Chooser.* Retrieved from http://creativecommons. org/choose/.

Chapter 2

Toward Participatory Pedagogy

Steve Hargadon, creator of Classroom 2.0 and the host of The Future of Education podcast series, illustrates the effect of our 21st-century life, peppered with social technologies, as a massive wave.[1] If you take a moment to imagine the image of a large wave in your mind, the way you naturally construct your vantage point may communicate how you feel about emerging technologies, as well as your level of current participation. Do you picture that wave about to hit shore and destroy everything in its path? Are you cautiously watching it from a protected balcony? Or are you riding it, shrieking with excitement as its energy throws you off balance?

Riding the wave with expertise surely isn't everyone's objective, but if you're reading this book, you clearly have some interest in submerging yourself a bit further. Typically, one of the most overwhelming elements of teaching with emerging technologies is deciding which tool or tools you should try. Note that I say, "try." Teaching with emerging technologies is, by nature, experimental, and failure is an implicit step in an experiment. If we don't fail, we don't learn, and if we don't learn, we won't improve upon what we're already doing. And in the 21st century, improving upon a centuries-old tradition of teaching and learning is critical.

Still, failure is tough. And professors don't openly relish the opportunity to fail. Why would we? Professors are products of an educational culture that has taught us to discourage failure, to be ashamed of mistakes, to always be right. Grades are presumably evidence of successful learning, and that relished 4.0 grade point average certainly doesn't include room for any failures at all. Low grades follow students, tarnishing their GPAs and reducing their opportunities to apply for scholarships and other merit-based achievements and opportunities. The modern educational system and, in turn, Western culture defines failure as something bad that should be avoided at all costs.

Ironically, brain research tells a much different story. Take a moment to reflect on something you are good at—cooking, painting, gardening, computer repair, fishing, negotiating, debating—anything. Think back to your experiences over the years, as you grew and developed your skills and expertise in this area. First, you wouldn't have had a chance to develop your skills only through reading about how to be proficient in this skill. You had to actively participate and give it a try. And as you reflect back on your growth, what was it that enabled you to improve? It was probably a new dish that tasted horrible, a color combination that looked garish, a computer screen that didn't go on when it should have, the big fish that got away, a lost deal, a failed argument . . . you get the picture.

Now you might agree with that point when we consider it in the context of personal hobbies or everyday skills, but what about in your teaching? What motivates you in your role as a college instructor? How do you view your role in a classroom? Is it important to you to see your students succeed? Each college instructor will respond to these reflective questions differently, and your response will provide valuable insights about your teaching paradigm.

Barr and Tagg's insightful article from 1995, "From Teaching to Learning," explores the characteristics of two distinct paradigms that operate in various ways throughout higher education: the teaching paradigm and the learning paradigm. Figure 2.1 provides an illustration of these two paradigms. Applying

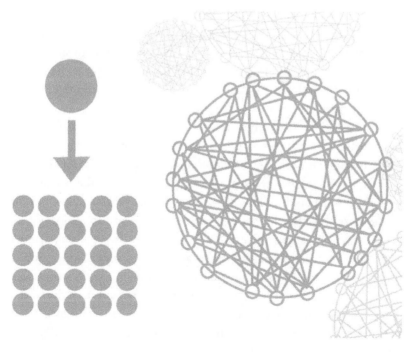

Figure 2.1 Lecture and participatory learning models. Image by Laurie Burruss. Reproduced with permission.

Instruction Paradigm	Learning Paradigm
Transfer of knowledge	Elicit discovery & construct knowledge
Cover material	Design learning environments
Lecture	Facilitate learning experiences
Achieve access for diverse groups	Achieve learning for diverse groups

Figure 2.2 Instruction and learning paradigm charts.

these ideas to your own classroom is an illuminating experience, as it encourages you to examine your teaching values and philosophy.

I find it helpful to imagine Barr and Tagg's instruction and learning paradigms at opposite ends of a continuum. Take a moment to review a few of the characteristics of each paradigm listed in Figure 2.2, reflect on your own values and motivation, and identify where on the continuum your teaching lies.

Emerging technologies hold an array of opportunities for teachers committed to achieving the outcomes of a learning paradigm. By nature, social media, Web 2.0 tools, and mobile apps are participatory and easy to use. In short, they create a cascading array of opportunities for students to be active contributors in the learning process, yielding fabulous ideas for assessments and strategies for increasing student interaction.

It's also a good practice to identify where on the continuum the institution(s) at which you teach lies. Institutions demonstrate their priorities through policy and decision making, and often, an instructor who values the priorities of a learning paradigm but teaches at an institution committed to the instruction paradigm finds him or herself in a challenging situation.

I shared the Barr and Tagg model in a presentation I gave to a mostly faculty audience at a very large public university, and the Twitter backchannel (a stream of real-time brief messages sent by audience members from mobile devices in response to my presentation) included comments from instructors that questioned whether or not their institution would ever embrace the learning paradigm. The evidence they cited for this was the large size of their classes. The more students there are in a class, the more challenging it is to adopt the priorities of a learning paradigm. For example, designing a learning environment in a philosophy class that is targeted at eliciting discovery, constructing knowledge, and achieving specified learning results for a diverse student group requires an instructor to engage with students, have an understanding of who the students are, have a willingness to adapt and shift the direction of activities in response to the group's unique needs, make necessary accommodations for special needs within the group, and make an effort to arrange course content in a variety of ways including text, image, and video. The more students there are in a class and the more classes an instructor teaches, the more difficult it is for an instructor to master the learning paradigm, regardless of his or her personal teaching preferences and values.

Be creative! There are practices in motion that demonstrate how emerging technologies can introduce more active learning into even very large lecture classes. Elizabeth Sowers, a sociology professor at California State University, Channel Islands, was reluctant to integrate technology into her face-to-face Introduction to Sociology class, which enrolls about 100 students. She reflects, "I was worried that encouraging students to use technology in the classroom would lead to them checking out, surfing Facebook, or playing games rather than listening to the lecture . . ." Despite these hesitations, Sowers made the choice to try TopHat in her class (see Chapter 5 for more about TopHat). TopHat is a next-generation student response system. It is used similarly to how instructors have used "clickers" in classes to capture student feedback and assess knowledge during a lecture, but TopHat operates on a student's own device (smartphone, tablet, or laptop). With her eyes set on increasing student engagement, Sowers has used TopHat for comprehension-check questions, opinion questions, data interpretation questions, and as a way for small groups of students to report back after a breakout activity. TopHat has had a surprisingly positive impact on student engagement, says Sowers, citing that her students express appreciation for the opportunity to check their comprehension on topics; students find the opinion questions fun, because they provide opportunities to understand how their perspectives compare to those of their peers; and the use of TopHat, in general, breaks up the experience of listening to a lecture, which helps to keep them engaged.[2]

As products of our educational system, professors have traditionally been positioned as the experts with all the answers. Experimenting with new technologies in your teaching will require you to step into a new teaching paradigm that encourages and fosters a community of learners who are incentivized to work together and solve problems.

So expect to fall off that surfboard a few times as you begin to teach with emerging technologies, but view each of those slips as opportunities to grow and cultivate more effective, relevant learning experiences for your students.

The Value of Participating

Ana Maria Barral started her career as a research scientist. After many years working in the private sector, she walked away from her title and security to teach college biology classes. It didn't take long for Ana to realize how scarce full-time faculty positions are and see that her new life, at least for the interim, was going to involve teaching classes at a variety of colleges and universities.

During Ana's transition, she found herself feeling as if she had lost her identity. She went from a formal title and institutionalized role to being affiliated with several colleges and not feeling like part of the "full-time" community at any of them. In an effort to improve her teaching, she registered for a face-to-face, technology-based workshop. That face-to-face workshop gave her the skills to create video lectures that she could use to web-enhance her biology classes. But it also piqued her curiosity about technology and teaching and gave her the self-confidence to try new things.

Not long after that, Ana enrolled in my Building Online Community with Social Media class. This is a fully online class I taught for the @ONE Project, the same program that funded Ana's Camtasia workshop. @ONE is funded by a grant from the California Community College Chancellor's Office and offers professional development classes designed for community college instructors but used by K–12 and higher-ed faculty from across the nation. In the class, instructors experimented with an array of social technologies and worked together in participatory environments to discuss and evaluate how the tools can be applied to online classes to foster a sense of community among learners. The first interaction I remember having with Ana was the week the participants were asked to create a Twitter account and start tweeting. She wrote to me expressing concerns about privacy and social media. In our exchanges, we talked through those concerns, and I told her she shouldn't do anything she isn't comfortable with, but I wanted her to give it a shot. My advice was simple: don't share anything private (advice every user of social media should take to heart). Soon thereafter, I saw her first tweets surface. They continued with more and more frequency through the end of the class.

In the months that followed, Ana used Twitter to share resources she stumbled on but also to follow research biologists, organizations, and educators around the world, many of whom followed her back. Quickly, her social media participation enabled her to curate her very own global network of users with shared interests. This Personal Learning Network (PLN) has changed Ana's life. Ana shared that while she was teaching for multiple institutions, her sense of isolation diminished as her use of social media increased. She has found a sense of community, a feeling of belonging—but also cultivated a dynamic network of individuals who she exchanged relevant teaching ideas and resources with and received help or advice about teaching-related problems.

Today, Ana still uses Twitter and has about 1,500 followers!

However, tweeting wasn't Ana's only venture into the world of social technologies. She also became a blogger. She uses her blog as an open space to work through teaching experiments—writing about her ideas, summarizing her experiments, and then reflecting on how things went. For example, in her post, "From Boring to Blogging, Part 3," she shared her newly created rubric for scoring her biology students' reflective blog posts that captured the scaffolded development of their research. Her blog has opened her teaching process to the world, allowing anyone to learn with her through her journey into teaching with emerging technologies. In the summer of 2016, Ana began a crowdfunding campaign (an online effort to raise funds through the use of social technologies) to raise money for a research project to explore the microbes attaching to floating plastic in coastal waters. A long-term goal of the study is to crowdsource data collection by having students and community organizations submit plastic samples from local waters.

I asked Ana how her teaching has changed since she first embarked on her use of Twitter. She said she feels like her teaching has transitioned from "black and white to full color." "When I teach now, I feel like I am serving my students a buffet rather than a quick bite to eat." She reflected on the ways that social media and Web 2.0 tools have potential to engage more students and extend confidence to learners who are traditionally marginalized through lecture and exam-oriented classes. "More of my students feel good about themselves."

This transformation did not occur without challenges. At one point, Ana was interested in encouraging her students to use their mobile phones to take pictures in their lab and use the images for web-based blogging and other assessments, but her department at one of her institutions had a strict policy against use of cell phones in class. As a part-timer, these institutional policies were difficult to negotiate. In higher education, there are many traditionalists who do not see the value of turning a phone into a learning tool. Like psychologist Abraham Maslow said, "If you only have a hammer, you tend to see every problem as a nail."

As a veteran researcher, Ana shared some intriguing perspectives about the broader implications of social media in the field of research. She noted,

> We used to just have peer-based research journals to share our findings. Today, we still have them but social media provides us with a space to experiment with global input. My blog and my Twitter users play a role in

helping me work through my problems and learn from my failures. In the end, everything will be kicked up a few notches. It's exciting.

Since the start of her teaching transformation, Ana was tapped by Carnegie Mellon to participate in a national review of an open online biology course, and she has been hired to teach biology full time at National University.

Integrating social technologies into your teaching has potential to transform your pedagogy from linear transfer of knowledge to interconnected participatory inquiry. However, this journey begins with your active participation. Reluctance and vulnerability are natural responses to stepping into the social media arena. However, you will find that your efforts to embrace your vulnerability and try new things will open new pathways for your teaching as well as your own lifelong learning.

Getting Started

After you have experientially learned the potential that emerging technologies hold for your students' learning, you'll want to understand how to get started with integrating them into your teaching. This chapter provides a list of criteria for evaluating individual tools for use in your own teaching. Before we dig into the evaluation criteria, there are a few critical elements you should flesh out to eliminate messy surprises down the road.

Take some time to reflect on the following questions.

What Function Will the Tool Serve in Your Class?

Identifying the function the tool will serve is essential and stresses a critical message about teaching with emerging technologies: a tool should always be used *in support of* pedagogy.

This first step may be difficult and, honestly, you may not have a crystal-clear response to it at first but you are likely have some idea. Take some time to reflect on this question and even write a few paragraphs about how you envision your students' experience or your teaching approach to be enhanced or altered by an emerging technology.

Three common functional uses of emerging technologies in learning are as follows:

1. enhancing interaction between you and your students and/or between students themselves (see Chapter 4)
2. creating online content for your class—for example, online presentations, demonstrations, lectures (see Chapter 4)

3. creating a learning activity that integrates student-generated content and/ or participatory learning (see Chapter 5)

If you are seeking a tool to facilitate a learning activity, you should keep some solid groundrules in mind about instructional design:

- Start with clear, measurable learning objectives.
- Select a tool that accommodates your objectives and is appropriate for the tasks or skills to be learned.
- Align your use of the tool with these objectives.
- Develop a rubric to assess your students' work.

Who Will Use the Tool?

Will the tool be used exclusively by you (for example, to create communications for your students or lecture content), or will students also use it (to create their own presentations or interact in a peer-to-peer learning environment, for example)?

If students will use the tool, you should plan to do the following.

Provide How-To Instructions

Clear instructions must be shared with students from the start. These may very well already exist. Don't hesitate to share online instructions with students, especially if they're provided on the tool's website.

Part of teaching with emerging technologies is responding to frequent updates and redesigns of tool interfaces and new enhancements. Therefore, relying on external help resources will lighten your load. You should only develop your own instructions to enhance and refine existing instructions. Think ahead, anticipate changes, and build a plan to save yourself time.

Also, search for instructional "how-to" videos in YouTube (you will likely find more than you imagined!) or consider creating screencasts (covered later in this book) that provide visually illustrated steps of how to use a tool. If you create screencasts, consider breaking up the process into short one- to two-minute steps rather than one long "how-to" video. This enables students to focus easily on the step they have a question about and also facilitates easier updating later on.

Finally, consider sharing the content you develop on your blog, website, YouTube, Twitter, etc., with a Creative Commons license. Give back to the community that helps you.

Explain the Purpose

Along with "how-to" instructions, explain to students *why* you have integrated this tool. How will you use it to enhance their learning or increase their communication with you and/or their peers? As noted in Chapter 1, students appreciate understanding the context of a new tool when they are asked to use one.

Build in Opportunities for Student Feedback and Use Results to Make Improvements

At the end of the course, survey students to evaluate how effective their learning experience was with the tool. Did it achieve the function or objective you had in mind? A scale combined with open-ended questions is an effective approach to measuring the effectiveness of the tool.

TIPS FOR FEEDBACK

Google Forms for Quick and Easy Student Surveys

A Google Form (see Chapter 5 for more information) is a multipurpose tool. First, it's a quick, intuitive, and free option for crafting surveys with visually pleasing themes that can be shared easily via a link, email, or embedded on a website. Second, the responses are compiled in real time into a Google Sheet for easy viewing and evaluating. Responses can be viewed line by line in the online spreadsheet, or you can view a visual summary of them if you prefer.

Get started with Google Forms at google.com/forms/about.

AnswerGarden for Simple Feedback

Sometimes a survey is more than you need. If you're looking for a quick, simple tool that you can embed into your course or website just to get a quick pulse check from your students about an issue, content, tool, or new activity you're trying out, consider AnswerGarden. Deemed a "scribble space" by its creators, it is a simple and flexible tool that can be used for feedback or for brainstorming. There are two steps in an AnswerGarden:

1. Create a new AnswerGarden by submitting a question or statement. From my experiences, you will have more success if you prompt your students to respond in "one word." You do not need to create an account, but you are advised to include a password for your AnswerGarden so you may edit it later if necessary.
2. Share the link to the empty AnswerGarden with your students or embed it in your course or website.
3. Students submit their answers by typing their response into the box (no sign in is required), and their answers appear below the question in the form of a word cloud.

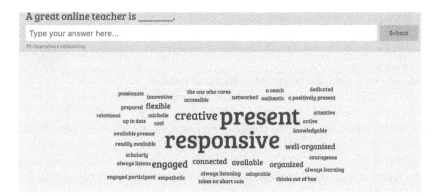

Figure 2.3 AnswerGarden screenshot. Used with permission from Creative Heroes.

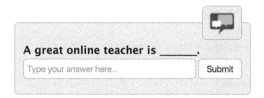

Figure 2.4 MicroGarden screenshot. To toggle to the AnswerGarden view, a user simply clicks on the logo in the upper-right corner. Used with permission from Creative Heroes.

The more frequently a response is received, the larger that word appears. You can sit and watch their responses grow your AnswerGarden (Figure 2.3)!

4. Sometimes you may find that you do not want your students to see the previous responses to the question, as this may influence their ideas (this depends on the nature of your question or statement). If you prefer to hide the responses, but still make them viewable with a simple click, try MicroGarden! It is a smaller interface, which is easier to embed on pages/sites that have limited space (Figure 2.4).

To get started with AnswerGarden, go to AnswerGarden.ch/.

SHOWCASE

Here is an example of how Julia Parra, assistant professor at New Mexico State University, uses Google Docs to integrate Web 2.0 tools into her classes to promote effective online student collaboration and group work.

She has students complete a "Sample Communications & Group Work Form" to identify the type(s) of mobile devices and media technology (webcam, video recorder, or audio recording device) students possess. She also assesses the students' self-perceived strengths (I am often the leader/editor/researcher in a group. I am good at creating multimedia. I am good at creating web-based media). To view this form, go to goo.gl/qRXKlg.

Parra leverages this information to implement group work and particular tools that best support the students in each group. She is able to organize the students into groups more effectively by evenly distributing the self-identified leaders, editors, researchers, and multimedia and web specialists.

At the end of the term, she implements a post-assessment to evaluate how the selected emerging technologies worked to support collaboration as well as gather the students' overall satisfaction with the tools.

When asked how the results of the survey were used in support of future online classes, Parra said,

> [The results of this survey] confirmed my belief in the importance of the process that I have formally developed and implemented in my online courses. I have always supported my students with the development of technology skills and provided some scaffolding for group work. However, the more formal process that I have developed is supportive in my overall process of online course design and is something that I can share with others.

How Will Your Workload Be Affected?

Encouraging students to create content with a Web 2.0 or social media tool is an effective way to assess learning, create relevant learning experiences more likely to foster deep learning, and develop critical-thinking skills.

However, if you are planning to have your students create content with social media or a Web 2.0 tool, plan ahead to ensure you have a clear understanding of how your workload may be affected. Here are some things to consider.

Your Participation Level

Effective, regular contact with your students is an important component of student success, especially if you are teaching online. Will your adoption of a new tool increase your need to actively contribute in your classes? Will there be additional areas where students may ask questions, for example, that you will need to monitor?

Class Size

The number of students in your class(es) will directly drive the amount of time it takes for you to monitor and evaluate the content created by your students. If you have large classes, think creatively about how you will assess the student-generated work.

Frequency of Assessment

How often will your students be using the tool? Weekly? Bi-weekly? Will you evaluate each student's work every time the tool is used?

 TIP!

The Nudge System for Grading Blog Posts

A blog is a terrific way to integrate reflective writing and other creative activities into your students' learning, but often professors feel overwhelmed by the need to assess every blog post. Here is a creative grading strategy that *may* help!

Let's say you assign a weekly blog post in three classes. Each class has 40 students in it. That means you have 120 posts to assess each week on top of other duties. Rather than telling your students you'll grade the blog posts each week, schedule two dates in your term when the blogs will be assessed—midterm and end of term work well.

Then, between the formal and comprehensive grading periods, inform your students that you will visit a handful of blogs each week to verify they are current, and you will leave comments for those students too (your comments will motivate your students and show that you are present). If you identify a blog that is missing a post, leave a "nudge comment" on the student's blog. The nudge is phrased something like this: "Your blog posts are looking great, but I am delivering a 'nudge' because you are missing our most recent post, [insert post title here]. We are all looking forward to seeing it soon!"

Each time a student receives a nudge, an automatic point deduction that will be incurred when the blogs are graded. It's a good idea to keep a simple list tally of nudges (perhaps on a spreadsheet used for grading notes). This is helpful just in case someone elects to delete your nudge comment.

The system worked well in my class. The deduction for a nudge was significant (5% of half the term's blog grade, so two nudges would drop a student an entire letter grade), and students who received nudges were very responsive and got back on track quickly.

Checklist for Evaluating Tools

After fleshing out your responses to the earlier questions, you may already be considering a few different tools. So how do you decide which one to implement in your class? There is no magical answer, but you will find that evaluating each tool against a set of criteria is a good practice to integrate into your workflow. Bethany Bovard's clean, useful "Web 2.0 Selection Criteria," which you can find at TekTrek.wordpress.com/2009/03/02/web-20-selection-criteria/, inspired the following checklist.

Accessibility: Can All Students Access the Tool or Content?

- Is the tool accessible by Windows and Mac users?
- Is the tool or content viewable in a variety of web browsers?
- Does the tool work well for those with dial-up connections?

- Does the tool provide options that support ADA compliance? If not, what are the gaps and how will you support them?
- Does the tool have a mobile app (or plans for a mobile app) for a variety of devices (iPhone, Android, iPad, etc.)?

Ensuring your course materials are accessible to all students, regardless of learning preference or difference, is an important priority for every instructor. In the United States, online course content must, by law, meet the criteria as outlined in Title II of the American with Disabilities Act, Section 508. When a face-to-face, hybrid, or online course utilizes static content (PDFs, Word docs, html pages, video files, etc.), the steps to fulfilling this criteria have been clearly established.[3] However, integrating emerging technologies into an online class can introduce quite a bit of murkiness, especially when those tools are being integrated with the explicit intent to foster learning through participation rather than through the traditional passive transfer of knowledge.

To understand the importance and value of accessible web content, University of Washington encourages you to consider the following:[4]

- Most individuals who are blind use either audible output (products called *screen readers* that read web content using synthesized speech) or tactical output (a refreshable Braille device).
- Individuals with learning disabilities such as dyslexia may also use audible output.
- Individuals with low vision may use screen magnification software that allows them to zoom into a portion of the visual screen.
- Many others with less-than-perfect eyesight may enlarge the font on websites using standard browser functions such as Ctrl + in Firefox and Internet Explorer 7 (Windows).
- Individuals with fine motor impairments may be unable to use a mouse and instead rely exclusively on keyboard commands, or use assistive technologies such as speech recognition, head pointers, mouth sticks, or eye-gaze tracking systems.
- Individuals who are deaf or hard of hearing are unable to access audio content, so video needs to be captioned and audio needs to be transcribed.
- iPhone users navigate the web using a small screen and touch interface on a device that doesn't support Adobe Flash.

The High Tech Training Center in California, which supports California's 112 community colleges, offers a helpful model for instructors to evaluate the accessibility of content, and it lends itself nicely to emerging technologies. Their model delineates "Three Cs" of accessibility: Container, Content, and Capability.[5] This model illuminates the multiple layers that need to be considered when evaluating a tool's ability to support all learners.

Container

Does the tool (i.e. the "container") support the use of assistive technologies (i.e. screen readers, text to voice dictation software, etc.)? If so, are there any features within the tool that do not support assistive technologies?

Content

Is content authored outside the tool and imported into the tool accessible to all (images, video, a mind map, etc.)? The accessibility of the content is separate from the container itself. And, as explained by Keegan and Brown, "while the container itself may not be fully accessible, the externally authored content can provide the information necessary for using assistive computer technologies."[6]

Capability

Is the container capable of supporting the creation of accessible content?

This evaluative step is a difficult one for professors, as it requires expertise that most professors do not possess. Individual institutions are responsible for establishing a process for course accessibility. This may involve professional development training opportunities, dedicated support, or a blend of these two. What's important is that you understand the resources that are available to you and that accessibility is integrated as a priority into the development of your course.

 **TIP!**

Web²Access (Web2Access.org.uk), a project of the University of Southampton in York, shares accessibility reviews of popular Web 2.0 and social media tools. The database of products that have been reviewed is robust, but the original reviews were conducted in 2009. Since then, the site has begun inviting the general public to submit reviews of Web 2.0 tools to maintain its usefulness. Many tools, however, have made substantive changes since their review, and there is no way to identify if these changes are reflected in the accessibility rating. Their ratings offer an excellent starting point for evaluating a tool's accessibility, and the criteria they use for their testing is openly shared on their site, providing a valuable tool for institutions to initiate their own evaluations (and share them!).

Be an Advocate for Accessibility

Finally, approach accessibility with an open mind and think outside the box. Some emerging technologies hold the potential to shift the paradigm of accessibility, creating new methods of reaching students through rich media. For example, to accommodate students who are hard of hearing, educators are traditionally encouraged to share captions for audio shared in an online setting. However, what if we could also include a video of a person signing that auditory content? Signing is the natural communication method used within the deaf community. Imagine how empowering that experience would be for students!

In your work, if you identify that a tool has value to your particular discipline but then realize that there are accessibility hurdles, don't run. Rather, reach out to your campus resources for support and advice about how to use it with accessibility in mind from step one. Also, reach out to the tool's developers and share your excitement and concerns. Engage in a conversation with them that offers an opportunity for them to listen and understand the needs of educators. You may or may not find them receptive to your needs and that will inform your thoughts about pursuing the use of the tool.

A Case Study: Emerging Technology and Accessibility

In 2007, I began experimenting with VoiceThread for teaching art history online. VoiceThread is a free web-based tool that provides a secure, participatory environment for discussing media through text, voice, or webcam comments. I was drawn to it because I felt unable to effectively teach a visually centric discipline in a text-centric course management system. Unlike an LMS, VoiceThread organizes conversations around media, flipping the traditional hierarchy of text to image. And users (that is, students) are extended the option to leave comments in text, voice, or video, cultivating an inclusive participation experience.

The first semester I used it, I noticed a few things. One, when given choices, students select the method that works for their individual needs. For example, I had a dyslexic student who excelled in the discussions when she elected to use her webcam to make comments, yet struggled endlessly to convey her idea through text. Two, I was empowered to *really teach* my online students through the feedback I was able to leave with my webcam and microphone. Rather than reading all my feedback in text form, students were given an opportunity to see and/or hear me, which enabled me to convey my excitement, concern, or pride about their work.

Despite all this wonderful inclusivity provided by VoiceThread, the tool itself was designed in a Flash "container." While Flash is installed in most web browsers (making it readily available to nearly all online students), it does not currently support the use of screen readers, an assistive technology used by students with vision impairments. I began a dialogue with the VoiceThread developers about my concerns and they listened—we actually scheduled a phone call at one point with an accessibility specialist to gather further evaluation about the hurdles that the product would present to users relying upon screen readers. Three years later, VoiceThread released VoiceThread Universal, a "back door" that provides access to VoiceThread content through an html, rather than Flash, container.

VoiceThread has also developed an option for license holders to integrate closed captions for caption central media (video or audio files that appear in the center of a slide) and voice/video comments (Figure 2.5). If your institution has a site license to VoiceThread, captions can be requested after integrating with a third-party captioning company (current options are 3Play Media and AutomaticSync Technologies). Institutions pay for the captions through a separate account set up with the captioning company, and designated individuals at the institution simply click on a CC icon to trigger the caption request. CSU Channel Islands currently uses

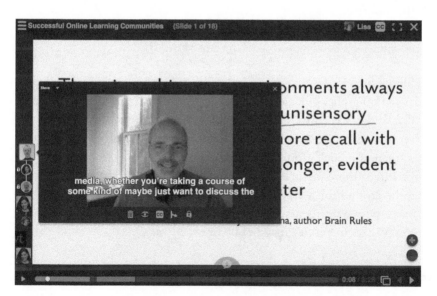

Figure 2.5 VoiceThread video comment with captions. Used with permission from VoiceThread.

VoiceThread's captioning process to provide accommodations to students with disabilities. To read CSU Channel Islands' VoiceThread Accommodations Plan for Students with Disabilities, go to TLInnovations.cikeys.com/voicethread-accommodations-for-students.

Learning Curve

• Is the tool easy to use?
• Are online support resources provided?

As you evaluate different tools, consider how challenging they are to learn. Reaching back to Chapter 1's focus, consider the student perspective. If students will interact in or create content with the tool, take extra caution in selecting tools that are intuitive. This will have a direct impact on the number of questions you receive. Seek out easy-to-use tools and evaluate built-in support resources. Remember, there will always be a learning curve, and your role is to motivate students, provide clarity about *why* they're using the tool, and point to clear instructions and help resources to support them.

Cost

• Is the tool free?
• Is there a premium version?
• Can your goals be achieved with the free version?

Free is always preferred—that goes without saying! Premium cloud-based technologies can offer phenomenal values through monthly or annual subscription rates. The days of expensive OS-specific software are behind us!

However, as many start-ups (and users of their products) have learned, "Free is not a business model." Tools that offer both a free and premium service are demonstrating a more mature revenue model. This is a sign that they are more likely to be around for a while, but there are never guarantees! Also, keep in mind that service agreements with emerging technologies are likely to change over time. What's free today may not be free next year.

Authentication

• Does the tool require all users to create an account?
• Does the tool offer a Learning Tools Interoperability (LTI) plug-in that allows for integration with your institution's LMS?

When a student is required to sign in to an online account before making a contribution or creating content in a tool, anonymous contributions are not permissible. That's important to you, as you will need to be able to identify contributions made by students in order to assign points for work (if you have decided that's relevant for your particular situation). So, on the one hand, requiring students to sign in is a good thing.

On the other hand, teaching with extraneous web-based tools that require students to create their own individual accounts and sign in each time they are used can also result in a rocky road for students. Imagine being a student enrolled in four classes, each requiring you to create two accounts for Web 2.0 tools. If all of those tools are unique, that is a total of eight accounts. These eight accounts could easily include three tools that essentially accomplish a similar function.

To ameliorate this type of scenario, it's important to be in dialogue with your colleagues in an effort to understand what other tools are being used—either as individual experiments, small pilots, or department-wide usage—to leverage existing knowledge and resources, and, ultimately, collaborate to produce a learning environment that is most effective for students.

Phil Hill, of Mindwires Consulting and co-publisher of the e-Literate blog, has described teaching with an LMS like teaching in a walled garden. But this is changing. Students learning in a class that incorporates web-based tools have typically had to click on links to open content in a new window, sign into the external tool, complete their work, and then come back to the LMS. Embedding content into an LMS has been the slickest way to create a more seamless experience for students—but doing this can be time-consuming, tedious work for instructors.

The IMS Global Learning Consortium (IMSGlobal.org), a non-profit consisting of educational institutions and suppliers of learning technologies, is changing the way institutional systems and learning technologies integrate with each other. This involves the development of interoperability standards and software to improve the teaching and learning experiences of instructors and students. Learning Tools Interoperability (LTI) is a standard developed by IMS that seamlessly integrates web-based tools within an LMS, improving the students' and instructor's experience. With LTI, students can log into their campus authentication system, access a course in their institution's LMS, and have direct access to activities and content from third-party tools without needing to sign in to additional accounts. Depending on the features a tool provider incorporates into its LTI, instructors may have the option to view and assess student work without leaving the LMS, score an assignment and have the scores populate directly into the LMS gradebook, and review analytics about student use and performance. In short, LTI provides seamless plug-and-play integration between institutional learning systems and external learning technologies without providing companies access to student data.

When evaluating technologies for teaching, you should explore tools' websites to understand if they offer LTI plug-ins. If they do, you will need to examine the licensing requirements to use them. Some tools provide the LTI plug-in at no cost, and others provide it as part of a site license.

End Product

* If using the tool to author content, what format options are provided for the final product? Html-embed code, URL, or export to file (.mov, .mp4, .jpg, .png, etc.).
* If you are producing files, do you have a method of hosting them?

If the tool is being used to author content or share content that is authored outside of the tool, what is the end product? If the product is a file (an image or movie file, for example), you'll need to determine a method for hosting it online and consider any size limitations that may guide your workflow. For example, if you plan to upload video files into an LMS supported at your institution, there is likely a maximum size that has been allotted for your individual use. Knowing this ahead of time is important to ensure that you develop an alternative hosting option or request more space if permissible.

Alternatively, if the tool produces a web-based product, you should take note of the output options. Does it share a link to your product (www . . .), does it provide html-embed code (codes vary but typically look like a long string of incomprehensible text like this: <iframe width="560" height="345" src= . . .), or both? Develop a plan for where you will share the link or embedded object (see Chapter 1 for a discussion about the value of embedding versus linking to online content).

Sharing Options

* Do you have options that allow you to restrict access to the content you create (private, unlisted, invitation only, public)?
* If you will be inviting a group of students to use the tool or access the content you've authored, is there an alternative to sending invitations through email (for example, an invitation link)?

Does the tool provide access options for viewing the content? Seek out tools that provide a variety of privacy settings such as the following:

Private

Content is viewable by you only; it cannot be viewed by other users and will not be retrieved through a web search.

Those Who Have the Link (Sometimes Referred to as "Unlisted")

Content is viewable by you and any other users who have access to the link; content will not be located through a web search. This option enables embedded content to be viewable in a protected learning environment (such as an LMS), but doesn't permit the content to be viewed by the general public. This is a useful sharing option, as the content can be easily shared only with students after they have authenticated as actively enrolled students in your class.

Those Who You Invite

Content is viewable by specific users you have invited. This may require students to "join" (and you to approve their request) and then sign in before viewing the content. This option should be used with caution, especially if the tool specifies that invites must be sent through email invitations. Spam filters typically "catch" these generic invitations, resulting in confused students who never received the invitation you sent. It also results in aggravated professors who find themselves managing lists of students who received and didn't receive the invitation.

Alternatively, many tools provide a process to invite users through "a link" and this works well! The key is to share the link in a place that is accessible only by your students. Emailing the link directly to your students is one option. If you have an established email relationship in place, it is unlikely that your email will be devoured by a spam filter. Another option is to place the link inside your course shell in an LMS or on a password-protected web page.

Public

Content is viewable by anyone and will be retrieved through web searches. There are many excellent educational reasons for encouraging 21st-century students to learn in the open web. Doing so fosters digital literacy skills and promotes opportunities for global collaborative projects—skills that are directly relevant to one's success in a digital society. However, don't expect students to *know* they are contributing in an open web environment. It is your responsibility to communicate this to them upfront, and, as noted earlier, it's an effective strategy to explain why you've elected a public sharing option for their learning environment. Tips and strategies for managing student privacy effectively in an online environment are included in Chapter 1.

Intellectual Property

- What rights do you have to the work you share through the site?
- What rights does the site have to share your work without your permission?

Social media and Web 2.0 tools will require you to accept Terms of Service (ToS) prior to your use. If your students are using the tool, they will also be required to accept the terms. Unfortunately, they may be dense and laden with legal jargon that is difficult to comprehend. However, it's important for you to make an effort to understand these terms, particularly the sections that explain how your content may be used and shared without your permission. Be aware that ToS can change frequently.

Typically, the ToS will cover acceptable behavior and content standards (no objectionable material, pornography, etc.), copyright guidelines (which will stipulate that you take responsibility for ensuring you own the copyright of the content you share and/or have the necessary permissions to distribute copyrighted content), disclaimers that release the site from certain liabilities (for example, the credibility of content shared on the site or responsibility for your content if it is lost in a data failure), a privacy policy (see "Privacy"), and intellectual property overview.

When examining the intellectual property criteria in a ToS, it's important to remember that companies seeking to promote their product own online tools. Therefore, it's common to see a statement that stipulates 1) that you (or the copyright owner) maintain the rights to the work you share on the site, 2) that other users must abide by the rights you have defined for your work, and 3) that the site has the right to reproduce your work for whatever it wishes (usually for marketing purposes). It's also important to understand that the ownership of companies change, which affects the ToS you abide by.

For example, I share many of my presentations on SlideShare, an online repository of presentations that conveniently converts a PowerPoint or Keynote file into an online Flash-based presentation. SlideShare is currently owned by LinkedIn, which was recently purchased by Microsoft. By creating my account, I agreed to the SlideShare ToS. When LinkedIn purchased SlideShare, I received a notification that the ToS had changed, and I had to agree to the new terms to continue to use my account. With the Microsoft acquisition of LinkedIn, another change is on the horizon.

Here is an excerpt from the "Rights and Limits" section of LinkedIn's ToS:

> As between you and LinkedIn, you own the content and information that you submit or post to the Services and you are only granting LinkedIn the following non-exclusive license: A worldwide, transferable and sublicensable right to use, copy, modify, distribute, publish, and process, information and content that you provide through our Services, without any further consent, notice and/or compensation to you or others.[7]

Here's a story that demonstrates this intellectual property clause in action. One time, I presented a talk at a conference titled "Teaching in the Age of Participation." This talk was supplemented with a slide-based presentation. Prior to the delivery of my talk, I uploaded the slides to SlideShare and shared the link to the presentation in two ways: 1) in a post on my blog and 2) in a tweet using the conference hashtag (a simple text sequence starting with # that allows for tweets to be indexed and organized into a stream for a group of users to easily follow, read, and reply to in real time).

When an audience member raised her hand and asked if I could share the presentation, I said, "I already have. You'll find it on SlideShare and the link is available on my blog and in the conference's Twitter feed." As the copyright owner of the presentation, I maintained my rights to the content I had uploaded. If anyone in the audience wanted to redistribute my work or use it in their own work, they would need to abide by my licensing stipulation that I added on the first slide and identified in the description on SlideShare. However, by using SlideShare, I agreed to the LinkedIn ToS, which simultaneously gave SlideShare permission to use my work. That afternoon I received an email notice that my presentation was the most viewed presentation in the "Education" category and was being featured on the SlideShare "Education" page. That's an example of how a company distributes content (often driven by the reviews of other users) to promote and market their site.

In the end, it was just more exposure for my own ideas, and I had no problem with that! In fact, it was really fun and exciting to watch my work tweeted, liked, and "favorited" by so many users. This social media experience, for me, helped validate the relevancy of my ideas and assisted me with sharing my approaches, opinions, and perspectives. However, it's often difficult for college professors to feel comfortable with sharing their work. Academic experiences have taught us to protect our ideas and channel them into respected peer-reviewed publications. This tradition, reinforced by tenure and other traditional incentives, can rub against the grain of the concept of openness and sharing—values that are central to social media.

Privacy

- What personal information is required to create an account?
- How is this information used?
- How are cookies used?
- Is this a tool you use or plan to use for personal use also?

Let's get this out of the way: social media has redefined the concept of privacy. When you sign up for a new tool, you are asked to provide information about yourself. Don't feel obligated to fill in every field. Rather, just complete the required fields and limit what you share with companies.

The ToS that you agree to before you use a tool clarifies how your "personal information" will be used and disclosed. Navigating this information on your own is, unfortunately, tricky and perplexing. I find myself scratching my head each time I dig into a privacy policy.

More tool providers are conveying their interest in protecting your privacy to the extent possible in the open web. One indicator of this trend is the use of "trust marks" that represent validation by an external privacy service such as TrustE (TrustE.com/). When you see a TrustE seal on a website, you can be assured that the site has demonstrated compliance with TrustE's high standards for protecting the privacy of their users.[8] However, it's not a foolproof process. Security is a constantly moving target in our digital world and as companies innovate, policies and standards must be continuously revisited and reworked.

Facebook, which bears the TrustE seal, has been criticized for how it collects and shares users' data. One issue that complicates things is that Facebook's default privacy settings have become more permissive over the years. As a result, some users' status updates and personal photos were made visible to the public without them even realizing it. There are still options to keep your profile and the content you share visible to only select groups (Friends or Friends of Friends, for example), but everyone is not aware when it's time to adjust these settings.

The types of data Facebook collects about its users and the ways that data is shared by Facebook has also been scrutinized. A Facebook user may understand that the photos and status updates he shares is data that Facebook will have access to, but he may not realize that Facebook also keeps track each time he uses a Facebook "service" outside of Facebook. Services include apps that provide the option to "log in with Facebook" or a simple Facebook "Like" icon placed on a web page. Facebook also operates a family of companies, including Instagram and WhatsApp, with which your data is shared to "improve the services" offered by those companies.

Ads and Cookies

Sites that are free *may* come with additional privacy hurdles. If a site is free and isn't generating money from a premium service, it's getting paid *somehow*, and it's usually through the ads you see permeating the pages. Ads are intrusive to any user's experience because they are simply distracting, but they're also intrusive to a user's privacy. It's good to get educated about how those ads work.

Within a site's Terms of Use, you will also see reference to the use of "cookies." A cookie is a piece of text-based information that is transmitted from a site's server and installed on your computer (in your web browser). When you return to a site, it examines your cookies, and if it finds familiar information, it will use it to refine what you see on the site. For example, cookies can be used to create customized lists of videos in YouTube based on your previous viewing patterns or a customized list of books on Amazon. Cookies do not carry viruses, but they can reveal personal information about your web activities that may violate your idea of privacy.

Here is an excerpt of YouTube's Privacy Notice explaining how a user's personal information is used:

> We use cookies, web beacons, and log file information to: (a) store information so that you will not have to re-enter it during your visit or the next time you visit YouTube; (b) provide custom, personalized content and information; (c) monitor the effectiveness of our marketing campaigns; (d) monitor aggregate metrics such as total number of visitors and pages viewed; and (e) track your entries, submissions, and status in promotions, sweepstakes, and contests.[9]

So what's the big deal about cookies? They *are* useful and can customize your experience in a pleasant way, but when you're using tools that are proliferated with advertisements, the benefit of cookies can crumble. (Sorry, couldn't resist that one!) When you click from site to site online, you are making a choice to visit particular websites. What you may not realize is that many third-party sites also interact with you. This third-party site interaction is not transparent and, therefore, most of us are unaware that it is occurring until we see ads appear that relate to products or services we've searched for online.

 TIPS!

Lightbeam: To get informed about how third-party sites are interacting with you online, you may wish to try a Firefox Add-On called Lightbeam (formerly called Collusion). Lightbeam operates in Firefox and creates a real-time visual graph of third parties that are collecting your information as you browse the web. After I began running Lightbeam, I visited three sites (Facebook, Google, and Zappos) and Lightbeam indicated that a total of 21 third-party sites had interacted with me. Wow!

Go incognito: When browsing, open a private or incognito window in your browser to search anonymously. Any sites you visit within that window will treat you as a user that is not logged into any services. In other words, cookies won't be available to feed third-party sites.

Navigating the terrain of privacy in a digital, mobile society feels like falling into a rabbit hole. As users, we have responsibilities. As noted, it is important to review your account settings periodically, particularly the "privacy" sections. Beyond this general rule, when creating a new social media account (Facebook, LinkedIn, Twitter, or Google+, etc.), make a choice about *who* you will be when you are participating from that account. Are you Professor Rodriguez— Latino/a history scholar and department chair? Or are you Pedro—lover of microbrews, skydiving, your three kids, church, and dog, Chewbaca? Or are you both? If you're choosing to use a particular tool for professional *and* personal use, consider creating two accounts.

For me, I use all my social networks as a professional space to share ideas, resources, and research related to educational technology and online teaching, except for Facebook. Facebook is my social playground. For this reason, I maintain secure privacy settings on my Facebook account, and I include a note on the "About You" section of my Facebook profile that says, "I enjoy Facebook as my true 'social' network. It's where I enjoy being myself with my friends and family. If you are a professional colleague or a current student of mine, I'd love to connect w you on LinkedIn or Twitter (@brocansky). Thanks!" I'm clear about why I use Facebook, and I'm also particular about whom I befriend. And when I see a video of a cute puppy, I make a choice to share it on Facebook rather than Twitter. Remember, despite the complexities about privacy in our digital society, you have control over what you share and where you share it.

After reading this section, you may be feeling overwhelmed and trepidatious about the idea of using emerging technologies in your classes. You should try to view this information as knowledge that will make you a more informed and effective teacher as well as a 21st-century citizen. Navigating web pages and joining new online services is part of our life now. Chances are, after finishing this chapter, you'll become much more aware of how frequently you encounter ads online—even when doing something as simple as checking your email. Privacy is one of many threads in the fabric of teaching with emerging technologies, and you should consider it, along with all the rest of the threads, as you evaluate tools for use, but it should not act as a roadblock for achieving your goals.

21st-Century Skills

Growing up in a mobile world fosters drastically different perspectives about participation, privacy, credibility, and identity. When my son was 10, he asked me if he could share a video of him with his friends that I had posted to my YouTube account. I said, "Sure," and went ahead and uploaded the video for him. Then I told him, "I shared your video as 'unlisted,' which means your friends won't find it in a YouTube search. But you can just send the link to them." He stared at me blankly and asked, "What's the point of sharing a video on YouTube if people can't find it?" To his generation, getting "views" is a sign of social validation. Unfortunately, he wasn't born with a filter. He has learned how, when, and why to share content publicly as he has actively participated in sharing videos on YouTube throughout his adolescence under the tutelage of his (sometimes nervous) mom. Guided participation allowed him to begin to understand what content is acceptable for the public, what content should be kept private, and what content needs approval or permission from others before it can be shared publicly. As I read and discussed the comments of other users with him, we both developed standards of acceptable and unacceptable ethical activities, and evaluated the effects of both on a user's credibility.

Our digital information society has transformed the skills that are necessary to live a successful life. Twenty-first-century citizens are expected to be able to search for and evaluate digital information (which now exists in text, image, and video), synthesize ideas, and construct opinions, as well as analyze and respond to viewpoints in an ethical way. These skills are fostered most effectively through experiential learning. This is one of the most important outcomes of teaching with emerging technologies.

Often, the dialogue around 21st-century skills is set within the context of teaching youth. However, higher education is a critical step in achieving new media literacies. Students come to college for a variety of reasons, but central to all is an interest in preparing themselves for a successful, meaningful life. The environment—the outcomes, content, activities, and tools used to orchestrate them—plays a critical role in achieving this goal. If students spend their college years passively listening to live lectures in a brick-and-mortar room, there is little to no opportunity for new media literacies to be acquired. If professors are encouraged, inspired, and incentivized to teach with emerging technologies, the playing field will shift, and college will play a formative role in mastering necessary 21st-century skills and encouraging students to develop a credible digital footprint, which will play an important role in an individual's personal and professional success long after college.

Researchers from Harvard, MIT, and USC have produced a helpful case-book that contains curricular material for developing "new media literacies." The resource, "Our Space: Being a Responsible Citizen in the Digital World," (TheGoodProject.org/toolkits-curricula/our-space/) is shared online with a CC license, meaning the material is free to use as long as the author is attributed. It is openly available for educators to adopt and integrate into their own curriculum and professional development programs. Resources like this one not only extend opportunities for lifelong learning to self-motivated college educators but also signal important new curriculum topics for institutionalized professional development programs.

Teaching effectively with emerging technologies requires more than fluency in how to "use a tool." It also requires one to be able to demonstrate how to participate ethically and responsibly in online communities, evaluate the role that online self-expression plays in the formation of one's identity, analyze the opportunities and risks involved with online participation, and assess the credibility of online users and content. This is a complex topic that is vital to the future of higher education and the lives of our students.

Summary

This chapter serves as an important transition for us. It discusses the transition from teaching to learning, drawing from the work of Barr and Tagg, which serves as a framework for this entire book. As you make your journey from delivering content to crafting and facilitating participatory, student-centered learning experiences, you will leverage the tool evaluation criteria included in this chapter. In Chapter 3, you will be provided with a set of "essential" tools to get started and keep moving fluidly through your journey.

Notes

1. Hargadon, S. (2011, June). *Open Learning: The Future of Education* [Keynote presentation]. Online Teaching Conference, Orange Coast College.
2. Sowers, E. (2016, May 6). *Student Engagement in Large Lecture Classes: Teaching and Learning Innovations at CI* [blog post]. Retrieved from http://tlinnovations.cikeys. com/uncategorized/student-engagement-in-large-lecture-classes/.
3. For a succinct checklist to assist with evaluating web-based content for 508 compliance, visit www.epa.gov/inter508/toolkit/508_compliance_toolkit_web_apps. htm—checklist.
4. University of Washington, Web Accessibility. www.washington.edu/accessibility/ web.html.
5. Brown, C. & Keegan, S. *The Three C's of Accessibility and Distance Education, High Tech Training Center* [report]. Retrieved from www.htctu.net/publications/articles/ three_cs_111804.pdf.
6. Ibid.
7. LinkedIn. *User Agreement.* Retrieved on July 13, 2016 from www.linkedin.com/ legal/user-agreement.
8. View the TrustE program requirements here: www.truste.com/privacy-programrequirements/index.html.
9. YouTube. *Privacy Notice.* Retrieved on September 26, 2011 from www.youtube. com/static?hl=en&template=privacy.

Chapter 3

Essentials Toolkit

Tools are mere enablers. The journey you go on with a tool is what makes it powerful. In the flipped classroom case study shared in the introduction, I demonstrated how I leveraged online lectures and VoiceThread conversations to transform my students' learning. Again, the tools themselves are not important—it's the *experiences* they create that are critical.

The previous chapter provided you with a framework for evaluating tools prior to using them in your class. Chapters 3, 4, and 5 will introduce you to a variety of tools and identify examples of how they can be used. You should keep the evaluation framework in mind as you explore the buffet of tools I will present to you. Some may meet your criteria or spark new ideas for you.

The tools shared in the next three chapters are organized to convey how they can be used to achieve particular goals: to share content, to increase communications with your students, and to create participatory, collaborative learning activities. As you read these next few chapters, you will, undoubtedly, find more uses for them and expand upon the categories I've developed here—that's something to celebrate!

I consider the tools in Chapters 4 and 5 to be "second-tier" tools. They're powerful and important, but they work best when added onto an existing "essentials toolkit." The "essentials toolkit" includes a collection of hardware and software that you will use across the spectrum as you engage and participate in emerging technologies. Without these tools, my teaching would crumble.

Disclaimer: technology changes quickly. All descriptions of tools and account characteristics are reflective of services at the time of writing. Please refer to the website of each individual tool for current information.

Smartphone

Smartphones are handheld multimedia studios (I often wonder when we'll stop referring to them as phones). As you identify apps you use regularly on your computer (referred to as "web apps"), be cognizant of the fact that these web apps likely are available in the form of mobile apps too. The mobile version of a web app will, generally, be a pared down version with fewer options, but that is not always a bad thing. A simplified interface can mean a friendlier user experience. Having access to tools "on the go" opens a world of possibilities for you and your students. Scavify and Goosechase are apps that enable mobile scavenger hunts complete with customizable challenges and a leaderboard (which, essentially, tracks each participant's scores and shows who the leaders are). The VoiceThread mobile app enables opportunities for recording video comments from anywhere and capturing one's location as well as one's presence (see Chapter 5 for a great showcase about this strategy!). With the Zoom mobile app, you can participate in live video conversations from anywhere you have a connection. Additionally, a smartphone functions quite well as both a webcam and microphone, although I do not consider it a replacement for either.

 **TIP!**

Recording a video from your smartphone using the YouTube app is a simple and fast way to create, host, and share brief videos of yourself with your students. Imagine the impact of recording a brief module introduction video for an art history class in front of a painting in a museum or for an anthropology class in front of the chimpanzee display at a zoo. Handheld video recording can be great, but investing in a small tripod for your phone is a great strategy for composing higher quality recordings.

Webcam

 A webcam is an essential tool for teaching with technology today. Videos add your social presence to students' learning experiences and promote a stronger relationship between you and your students, particularly in online classes. A webcam can be used to record microlectures (see "Screencasting" in this chapter), personalized announcements (see "YouTube" in this chapter and the tip presented earlier), send video emails, and connect with students via synchronous webconferencing and communication tools (Skype, Zoom, Google+ Hangouts, etc.). You may already have a webcam on your computer—so be sure you check into that before you purchase one—but your built-in webcam may not produce high-quality results. You may wish to consider upgrading to an external high-def webcam for improved quality. When shopping for a webcam, I encourage you to peruse the CNET reviews to identify options that meet your needs. The higher the video output resolution, the better the image quality: CNET.com/reviews

TIPS FOR VIDEO RECORDING

Lighting Matters!

The right lighting conditions will transform the quality of the videos you record with your webcam. Many times users don't think about light and that can result in dark images that render your entire face in silhouette. What's the point of using a webcam if you aren't identifiable? A quick way to ensure you produce quality video with your webcam is to do your recordings with a light source in front of you, rather than behind or to the side of you. When light illuminates the front of your face, you'll be rendered beautifully on camera!

Look at the difference lighting makes in Figure 3.1.

What's Behind You?

When recording a video of yourself, it's easy to get consumed in your own appearance. But don't ever forget to examine the setting that appears behind you in your video. Take time to select a recording location that displays a neat and professional background (put away your dirty laundry or avoid sharing those vacation photos from your cruise on your wall!).

Figure 3.1 Webcam lighting comparison. Used with permission from VoiceThread.

Microphone

 A microphone allows you to communicate online with your voice, which may be more appropriate or convenient, at times, than video. Video conveys your physical appearance, including your gestures and facial expressions, and voice focuses on the qualities of your speech. Also, video files are much bigger than audio files. Think about these elements when deciding which output option is the best for your particular use.

Recording a video also requires much more preparation than recording audio. For example, when I use Skype I do not set it to pick up a call automatically with video because I want to be sure my surroundings are appropriate for my audience, and, let's face it, we're not always ready to present ourselves in video! However, I can easily use my microphone and engage directly in a voice-based conversation.

When purchasing a microphone, CNET reviews are a great resource to research your options. I recommend a USB microphone with a headset. This option creates high-quality audio recordings and also gives you the option to set your audio output to your headset, allowing you to hear more clearly and filter out background noise: CNET.com/reviews

Screencasting Software

 A screencast is a video recording of your computer's screen that is synced to the sound of your voice or video narration.

The uses of screencasting in teaching are endless—how-to videos, lectures, an orientation or tour of an online class. They provide quick and effective visual answers to questions, and students can create screencasts to demonstrate their ability to perform online tasks or to give presentations.

Not long ago, screencasting tools were expensive and using them required quite a bit of training. In short, just a few years ago, screencasting was for experts. Well, not anymore. Today, if you do not already have access to a premium screencasting tool (such as Camtasia or Screenflow), there are a number of free to low-cost tools that can get you on track for creating your own customized video content.

Screencast-o-matic.com

Screencast-o-matic is a free browser-based tool that gives you direct access to creating a screencast with a single click. The application launches a Java applet on your computer that runs the screencast. You click "record," resize the crosshairs to fit the size of your recording, select the microphone option you are using, indicate whether or not you want to also record from your webcam, click the record icon, wait for the countdown, and go! When you're done, click pause or stop, and then you have the option to upload the video to Screencast-o-matic's server, download it to your own computer (a variety of file options are provided), or upload it directly to your YouTube account. The quality of the videos uploaded directly to YouTube is impressive. Screencast-o-matic also includes the option to add "callouts" (visual enhancements that draw attention to your mouse clicks and make fine "how-to" details easier to see).

Account Details

Recording is possible without an account. If you create a free account, you'll be able to record videos up to 15 minutes in length and have access to your recording history. A Pro account includes premium features such as editing. Videos recorded with a free account will include a small watermark. Discounted group licensing options are available for groups of 10–2,500.

Jing—TechSmith.com/jing

Jing, a tool I use every day, is made by TechSmith, the creators of Camtasia and SnagIt. Jing requires a free download (available for both Mac and PC users) and produces screencasts up to five minutes as well as screenshots (still image captures of your computer screen). You can set the Jing app to launch each time your computer starts, and while it is running, a golden sun icon hovers at the top of your screen.

When you need Jing, simply activate it with your mouse, click on the "crosshairs" icon, and drag it across your screen to select the portion you want to capture. When you capture a still image of your screen, you can also annotate on top of the image (call out an area with a colored box, add a line of text, or include an arrow to point out something important). Then you may download the image or video file to your computer *or* upload it directly to your screencast.com account, which is automatically created when you install Jing.

Why is that important? Because in a matter of two minutes, you can create a one-minute video, upload it to the web in a click, and paste a link to the video in an email. That's what makes Jing so handy. It is irreplaceable when teaching online. I regularly use Jing to answer "how-to" questions, and I love hearing students' excitement when they realize I sent them a personally recorded video to answer their question. Responding to frustrated or nervous students with video is a great way to calm their nerves and support them through a class. See Chapter 4 for more about Jing.

Account Details

Jing is free.

Online Content Hosting Services(s)

Hosting your content online—"in the cloud"—empowers you to access your content from anywhere, share it easily without emailing large files, and facilitate virtual collaboration projects. Having video-hosting and document-hosting tools in your toolkit is essential.

YouTube.com—Free Online Video Hosting

 A free YouTube account provides you with a free hosting resource for video content *you create* and a personal channel that you can use to curate video playlists around focused topics that can be shared with relevant audiences.

- Each video you upload can be set to Public, Unlisted (which means only those who you share the link with can view it), or Private (you identify the individuals who may view it).
- YouTube limits your videos by length (which, at the time of writing, is 15 minutes for most users).
- I use my YouTube account to host video announcements and screencasts (screen recordings) for my classes. This option enables me to customize the privacy setting of the videos and then embed them in my LMS or the website I am using for teaching (see Chapter 1 for an overview of linking versus embedding).
- When you "upload" a video, you may select one from your hard drive that you've already created, or you can use your smartphone or tablet to record directly to YouTube if you have the mobile app installed. YouTube no longer supports recording directly from your webcam on your computer.
- The videos you create can be captioned within a matter of minutes, as long as you have a transcript of your video (saved as a .txt file). If you don't have a transcript, you can edit the auto-captions generated by YouTube (be sure to edit these before you activate them on your video, as I've found very inappropriate language in auto-captions that was not spoken in the video!).

 TIP!

YouTube is more than a video-hosting site. I also use it to curate my YouTube content (including the videos I create and the videos uploaded by other users that I want to save and share). My personal YouTube account includes a "channel" on which users can view playlists I have curated. For example, I have one playlist titled, "Teaching with Emerging Technologies" and another titled "Daguerreotype and Calotype." As I find videos I want to save, I can add them to a playlist, and I can then share each playlist with the related group of users. I embedded the "Daguerreotype and Calotype" playlist in a unit within my online History of Photography class. I also have a playlist titled "History of Photography" where I share mini-lecture-like videos that cover specific topics and themes related to photography.

Each time you share a video on YouTube, you have the option to share it with a CC license or a traditional YouTube license, providing more opportunities to create a culture of open content and foster lifelong learning around the world.

SHOWCASE

San Diego Community College District has developed a useful and concise website titled "Get Real" that walks faculty through different scenarios for using video in a class, highlights the benefits of using video, provides links to helpful tools, provides a series of workflows for recording and hosting, and lists captioning options.
Check it out here: SDCCDolvid.org/getreal/.

Dropbox.com—Cloud-Based Storage and Content Backup

Dropbox is like a mobile Flash drive on steroids! It is an application that you install, for free, on your computer. Once installed, a Dropbox icon appears in your toolbar and acts as a separate disk storage location within your everyday workflow. For example, when I go to save a file, I have the choice to save it to my hard drive or my Dropbox folder (functioning the same way a Flash drive would). I can access all the files I save in my Dropbox folder from any device with an Internet connection, for example, a computer in my classroom or my iPhone (via the free mobile app). I can also select a folder or group of folders on my hard drive and have them continuously sync to my Dropbox folder, which is a terrific option for a "class presentations" folder, for example.

All the files you save on Dropbox comes along with a simple "share link," which you may copy and share with users of your choice in an email, in your course site, Twitter, etc.

Account Details

Dropbox has free and premium account options, including site-wide options that offer the ability to provide all faculty/staff and students with accounts. At the time of writing, a free account provides a user with 2 GB of online storage space.

 **TIP!**

Dropbox's File Request feature is a great way to easily collect assignments or media files from your students and then share them with the whole class. Essentially, the feature allows you to set up a link (with our without a deadline) which, when clicked, prompts users to upload a file based upon the description you provided. Those files are automatically uploaded to your own Dropbox. You may then copy the "share" link for that folder and include it in your LMS or course website.

A Method for Captioning Videos

As noted earlier, videos must be captioned to be compliant with federal ADA requirements. When you weave captioning into your workflow, you are establishing a process that makes web accessibility an essential building block in your teaching process. Some faculties are fortunate to have services on their campus that do captioning for them. Many are not and do it themselves. Here are a couple of free options.

YouTube.com

If you choose to create a free YouTube account and use it to host your own videos, you have a few options for adding captions. The captions will play on the video wherever it is embedded (provided the captions are turned ON by clicking on the CC button). For detailed instructions for adding captions, search for "captions" in the YouTube Help Center:

- **Upload a file.** If you have a text-based transcript of your video saved in a .txt file, choose this option. YouTube will quickly convert the file to captions that sync with your video.

- **Transcribe and set timings.** This feature allows you to play your video and type a transcript into YouTube's online caption tool. You will need to tweak the timing of each caption you enter to ensure it appears in sync with the video.
- **Use automatic captioning.** YouTube has cutting-edge speech recognition technology that you may use to generate captions. While this option sounds too good to be true, use it with caution. This technology is improving rapidly, but relying on this option alone will likely result in inaccuracies (and some inappropriate words too).
- **Captioning services.** There is a growing list of third-party captioning services that provide a direct integration with YouTube, allowing you to automatically request captions for your videos. If your institution has a license with a third-party captioning company (such as 3Play Media, AutomaticSync, or Rev), inquire about the possibility of submitting your YouTube videos for captioning. Here is a list of YouTube-Ready Captioning Vendors: YouTubeReady.dcmp.org/.

Amara.org

While YouTube allows you to add captions to videos *you've* created, there will be times when you need to add captions to videos others have created. That's when Amara comes in handy. Amara is a subtitling community, which means it provides you with tools to generate your own captions, allows you to invite others to help, and also provides "on-demand" services for professional captioning. After a video is captioned, it becomes available to all and may be embedded anywhere. You may also choose to download the captions or sync them to videos in your YouTube account and other third-party video services.

A URL Shortener

While the need for a tool that condenses the length of a URL (link or web address) may not be immediately apparent to you, it will soon enough! Many of the super cool web tools you'll learn about in the following chapters will enable you to create content that is hosted online. Unfortunately, the ease and convenience of these tools comes along with the nuisance of really long URLs. When you share links to your activities, presentations, etc., it may be more effective to shorten them first. Each tool below allows you to shorten links without an account or create an account to view a list and analytics of your shortened links.

- **Bitly.com**—If you create an account, you will be able to track analytics on the URLs you shorten. Bitly offers premium enterprise accounts that provide branding of shortened URLs, mobile deep links, which enhance the experience of users who click your links from mobile devices; additional analytics; a user management panel; and dedicated support.

- **Goo.gl**—Google's URL shortener. This is a great option if you regularly use Google applications. If you are signed into your Google account when you use Goo.gl, you will build an ongoing list of your shortened URLs that will also provide analytics about each one (number of clicks, referring sites, and general profile information about the user).

- **Tiny.cc**—Provides a useful bookmarklet you may install in your browser for quick access to link shortening. Without creating an account, you may customize your shortened link, which makes it easier to remember and share with others, and generate a QR code that users can scan with a mobile app and be taken directly to your site. With a free account, you can also edit your links (in case a URL changes), use tags to organize your links, and export your link analytics into a spreadsheet. A premium account is available for more robust analytics and customized domains.

Tools for Creating Graphics

Designing a visually pleasing environment is an important part of teaching an online or blended class. This means learning how to design graphics that you may use in your LMS or course site and share via social media. Social media can be an excellent way to promote one of your upcoming classes or a guest speaker on campus. The tools that follow will empower you to give your content a WOW factor (and you'll have a lot of fun with them too!).

Canva.com: Free Online Graphic Design Tool

 Creating a free Canva account provides you with access to thousands of images and icons you can incorporate into existing templates or start fresh with a blank canvas. Canva is perfect for simple graphics (such as a thumbs up icon for an announcement regarding the results of a class project, a bold arrow to draw attention to part of your assignment's instructions, or a photograph of your class with the date imprinted on it). When you are done with your design, download it as an image file and upload it directly into your course site or LMS, or you may share it via the link provided by Canva. Canva also works great for other types of graphics, too, such as event invitations, course banners (see the showcase that follows), posters, presentation slides, and more!

Account Details

Canva requires you to create an account, but it is free. Logging into your account will provide you with access to all the designs you've created in Canva. You may edit any design at any time. A free account will likely fulfill your needs, but you may wish to upgrade to a Canva for Work account, which is free for educators. This account option provides teams with the ability to create a brand kit to ensure designs adhere to specific color schemes and fonts, resize designs (which is very helpful), and other features. Canvas for Work is a good option for instructional design teams who support faculty.

 TIP!

A study by Buffer showed that tweets with images receive 18% more clicks, 89% more favorites, and 150% more retweets than those without images.[1] The next time you turn to your social media networks to promote an event, keep that in mind!

SHOWCASE

Canva is a great resource for faculty who wish to customize their course site with eye-grabbing banners. CSU Channel Islands' Teaching and Learning Innovations team has used Canva to develop a collection of course banners. Faculty may select their favorite option and request their own customized graphic for their courses. See Figure 3.2 for two examples, or go to this link to view the Custom Course Banners for CI Learn faculty request form: TLInnovations.cikeys.com/services/

Figure 3.2 Examples of CSU Channel Islands' Custom Course Banner service. Images were created with Canva and used with permission from Teaching and Learning Innovations at CI.

Summary

The toolkit outlined in this chapter is like a Swiss Army Knife for teaching with emerging technologies. If you skip this chapter and move right into the next, you'll be back to this page soon enough! The following chapters will begin to flesh out some of the popular ways emerging technologies are being used in higher education and showcase some innovative uses to spark your creative juices. Let's now dive into Chapter 4 and discover some easy strategies for using free to low-cost voice and video tools to add the human touch to your online content!

Note

1. *Buffer Blog*. Retrieved on July 19, 2016 from https://blog.bufferapp.com/the-power-of-twitters-new-expanded-images-and-how-to-make-the-most-of-it.

Chapter 4

Tools for Communication and Content Creation—Beyond Text!

At CSU Channel Islands, I facilitate an online teaching preparation program for faculty that consists of a 6-week online course. Many faculty who participate in the program feel skeptical about the quality of online learning. Not because they're concerned about content, but because they're concerned about what will happen to their classes if they aren't present. For this reason, we have designed the first portion of the program to focus on empowering faculty to learn how to foster a strong sense of who they are online, in addition to build relationships with me, the course facilitator, and their peers in a fully online environment. The title is "Humanizing Online Learning," and starting the program with this content is making a big impact on how faculty feel about online learning.

In the course, faculty engage with their peers in asynchronous video conversations using VoiceThread, create a one-minute "course bumper" video using Adobe Spark Video, and embed that video in a website along with their written reflections created with Adobe Spark Page. By the time the course is over, faculty have moved out of their comfort zones, stepped into the role of content creators, and overcome the anxiety that often comes along with speaking into a webcam and sharing that recording with others. Throughout the process, they're reminded that they are not perfect, and their flaws are what make them wonderful and special to their students. They make mistakes and learn that the world doesn't stop if they screw up; in fact, these mistakes are pathways to growth as online teachers.

Confronting our anxieties is a difficult thing to do, especially in a field that expects us to be experts. Brené Brown is an affective researcher at the University of Houston who has studied shame and vulnerability. From thousands of interviews with research subjects, she has found that stepping into the arena and confronting our vulnerabilities is how we, as humans, find connection with others and discover our authentic selves.[1] That may seem a little too warm and fuzzy for a book about teaching with technology, but from my experiences working with faculty, I have observed that when faculty take the hard road to confront their anxieties and move beyond the skills they know they're good at, they grow enormously. Skepticism is washed away with excitement, pride, and enthusiasm for teaching online. At the end of the humanizing course, one faculty shared,

> I knew that learning in a classroom was a social interaction, but for some reason, I left that at the door when I tried to teach on-line. . . . Now I get it! And, I have learned that there are so many simple (and free) tools on-line that can help me make the experience more personal and more social.[2]

The tools that are shared in this chapter will extend the opportunity to you to bring your human presence into your online class as well as create and share visually stunning presentations and other types of content with ease. Even if these are tools with which you are familiar or have heard of, I'm hopeful that I have contextualized them in an innovative way, thus opening up new ways of thinking about how technology can be used to enhance teaching and learning.

Zoom.us—Live Video Conversations

Feature Overview

- Free and premium account options—free account limits meetings to 40 minutes and 50 participants.
- Business licenses (minimum of 10 accounts) include an LTI plug-in for LMS single sign-on and a personal vanity URL for each host's meeting room.
- Host and participants have access to desktop and application sharing, including option to share the screen from one's iPhone or iPad.
- Meeting participants do not need a Zoom account.
- Built-in chat, participant list, and "raise hand" feature.
- Host-specific controls include polling, breakout rooms (allowing for small group interactions within a meeting) and control over participants (lock room, lock screensharing, mute microphones/video).
- Co-annotation on shared screen.
- Ability to take control of another participant's screen.
- Support for live captioning available.
- Option to insert virtual backgrounds using a green-screen feature.

Zoom is an excellent and easy-to-use program for hosting live video conversations. It's a terrific option for online office hours and group activities, and supports mobile devices, thus allowing for participants to join in from anywhere with an

Internet connection. In Zoom, the meeting host schedules the meeting using his or her Zoom account and sends a link to meeting participants. The participants click the link; download Zoom (only time only) onto their computer, or if they click the link from a mobile app they will be prompted to download the app; and the meeting opens. While participants do need to download the application, they do not need an account to participate in a meeting. This, to me, is one of the features that sets Zoom apart from other synchronous video tools. There is a very low barrier to participate. It works, and it's easy.

Once in a Zoom session, users can toggle between two views: gallery view (looks like a Brady Bunch configuration) and speaker view, which shows the active speaker large on the screen and the non-active speakers in smaller boxes along the top. There is a chat feature built-in for text communications. The chat content is downloaded to the host's computer as a .txt file when the meeting ends. The meeting host has the ability to initiate polls to collect data from participants and manage the participant list, from which she may mute/unmute participant mics/webcams and see if anyone has activated the "raise hand" feature.

Zoom's breakout room feature opens great opportunities for small group activities. The host simply clicks "breakout rooms"; indicates how many rooms are needed; chooses to manually assign participants to the rooms, or has Zoom auto assign the room members; and then activates the rooms when ready. The participants then magically disappear into their rooms. During the breakout room sessions, participants may request a visit from the host who can then pop into the room as needed. When the allotted time for the rooms is close to ending, the host gives the participants a 30-second countdown, and then everyone rejoins in the main room.

Also, there is a recording feature built into every Zoom account, and the host may give one or all participants permission to record the video too. This option enables students to drive the needs of their own learning. When recording is activated, the video file is downloaded directly to the computer of the user(s) who activated the recording. Those with premium accounts can also choose the cloud recording option, which auto-hosts the video online and sends an email to the host with the direct link.

 TIP!

Zoom works great for screencasting (videos of your screen with your voice narration) too. Simply start a new meeting with video, click "share screen," click record, and start speaking. The video will be downloaded to your computer, and you may then import it into a video editing program to clean it up or upload it directly to YouTube or another hosting service.

SHOWCASE

How Live Video Tools Open the Gateway for Mobile Guest Speakers

As educators, we all understand how inspirational it can be to connect students with guest speakers. Today's digital, mobile society now allows guest speakers from anywhere in the world to enter our classrooms without any type of travel. There are many tools that support the inclusion of mobile guest speakers in the classroom: Skype, Zoom, and Google Hangouts are three of my favorites. The inspirational story that follows provides a wonderful example of the motivational affect using technology to connect students with a subject-matter superstar can have.

Lori Rusch is a vibrant art history professor who teaches at multiple institutions throughout the Los Angeles area, including Rio Hondo College, Cal State LA, and she has also taught advanced level art history courses at Los Angeles County High School for the Arts. The story I am about to share here is one of the most inspirational stories I've heard regarding the use of technology in the classroom to empower student learning.

Rusch is a self-proclaimed "Freeway Flyer"—a term used frequently in California to describe the reality of part-time instructors who teach at multiple campuses (often with no office but their car trunks and limited access to campus resources), usually with little certainty about the existence of their jobs from term to term. I share this context because I think it's important to relate to the complexities and challenges that many faculty members navigate continuously while trying to meet the needs of their students. Despite these circumstances, Lori's commitment and passion to teaching and innovation in the classroom shines.

The event from her high school class that is shared here was not part of Lori's plan for her course—it was a spontaneous move to respond to an unexpected interest and enthusiasm that had bubbled up to the surface in her class as her students were shown excerpts of Nigel Spivey's video series "How Art Made the World." *Who* would ever imagine that an art historian could become a celebrity on a high school campus? Go figure. Rusch allowed her students' energy, curiosity, and wonder to flow naturally until one day, while listening to students enthusiastically mimic Spivey's English accent, she suggested, "Well, why don't you contact him and see if he'd chat with us?"

The students were stunned. Surely, Spivey seemed unreachable to high school students. He is, after all, a celebrity. They even asked, "Why would *he* want to talk to *us*?" Rusch contextualized things a bit and explained that Dr. Spivey is a real person and a real professor—a teacher—at Cambridge University, and if he is an educator, why would he *not* want to speak to a group of students? With conviction, a student asked, "Do you think we could do a video conference with him?" And that's how it all began.

In the coming weeks, the students worked together (again, remember *none of this* was for credit) to draft a letter to Dr. Spivey, which their teacher sent to him on their behalf at his Cambridge email address. Not long after, he accepted their invitation. Rusch suggested to him that the conversation be facilitated with Skype, and the two of them connected one time in advance to be sure the technology would be capable of managing an overseas video exchange (both users were utilizing the free version of Skype).

Meanwhile, to help accommodate the students' desire to work as a team to develop interview questions, Rusch elected to set up a Facebook page for the students who had accounts to use (most were already using the service). The students interacted between class meetings to collaboratively draft the interview questions for Spivey's virtual visit to their class. As the date grew closer, they also created posters for the event and began to hang them around campus.

The interview occurred on a Friday morning—two hours before the students' classes actually began. Colleagues shook their heads at the antics. One told Lori that she'd be lucky to "get two kids to show up." They were wrong, oh so wrong! Not only did students come, they packed the room. The students arrived to hear/see the interview because they were excited and inspired, *not because they had to be there*. All the myths and comments I've heard about students "these days" being apathetic and unwilling to do more than they're required to do are capsized by this story—which, I think, is why I love it so much! It crystallizes the difference a great teacher can make—one who is committed to being flexible to support, guide, and cultivate the fluidity of her students' energy through the process of learning.

The interview went without a hitch, except for a two-second delay before Spivey's video image appeared. The students, one after another (a few dressed in outfits that mirrored the attire that Spivey wore in his video series), approached the webcam and asked Spivey the questions they had prepared while the rest of the students watched and listened.

If you'd like to watch a partial video recording Rusch made of the interview as well as a presentation she created and shared on SlideShare, visit the Chapter 4 resources shared online at TeachingWithEmergingTech.com.

Piktochart—Engaging Infographics for Online and Print

 piktochart.com

Feature Overview

- Easy-to-use infographic creator with format options ranging from online graphic, presentation slide, report, or printable poster.
- Free account available. Results in watermark on your work and limits templates and privacy options.
- Deeply discounted individual educator and classroom accounts available. Benefits include removal of watermark, access to all templates, high-resolution image and PDF exports (for print), increased file storage for your own images, and enhanced privacy options.
- Includes a robust library of icons, charts, and maps for use in your work.
- Import your data from Microsoft Excel, Google Sheet, or Survey Monkey and render it in visual format.
- Free mobile app for iPad.

An infographic is an image that communicates ideas and/or data. Infographics are valuable resources when you are designing an online course. They support principles of Universal Design for Learning by offering a visual method of communication. Creating infographics, however, is not an easy task. It requires access to existing icons and visual imagery that is properly licensed for re-use, in addition to keen design skills. Piktochart is an online tool that makes creating infographics easy.

The free account is robust enough to support any beginning creator of infographics, but if you really want to embrace their power, upgrade to the individual educator account. Not only will it eliminate the branding watermark but also provide you with more options for managing the privacy of your work and allow you to export the graphics into high-quality and printable formats.

When you (or your students) create an infographic, consider including a CC license in the work so it clearly communicates to others how you permit its re-use. I created an infographic using my Piktochart educator account that identifies six tips for recording video. Knowing it would be valuable to other educators, I shared the graphic with a CC-BY license, which allows others to re-use it and adapt (or remix) it to fit their own needs, provided they attribute me in their re-use of the content.

Figure 4.1 Infographic created with Piktochart. By Michelle Pacansky-Brock, CC-BY.

 TIP!

Like many other tools highlighted in this chapter, Piktochart is an ideal way to challenge students to demonstrate knowledge of an issue in a visual and concise manner. If your class includes a required research paper, you may wish to incorporate one or both of the following options as alternative student assessment methods:

- Produce an infographic that accompanies the report, communicating a position on the issue backed up with data. Require students to share their infographic on at least one social media network of their choice and have them include a screenshot of that share along with their report and infographic.
- Develop a website (using Adobe Spark Page, Populr, or a tool of their choice) that includes an abstract of their report, a link to the report, and an embedded version of their infographic.

When incorporating data into an infographic, sources must be cited in the graphic (at the bottom, in footnote fashion) to ensure the graphic is credible.

Jing—Visual Communications

   TechSmith.com/jing

Feature Overview

- Facilitates seamless creation, hosting, and sharing of screenshots and up to five-minute-long screencasts with a simple link.
- Free application that requires installation on your computer (PC or Mac).
- When you install Jing, you simultaneously sign up for a free screencast. com account on which your Jing screencasts (videos) and screenshots (images) are hosted (when you select this option).
- Jing is a TechSmith product (creator of SnagIt and Camtasia).

I actually included Jing in the Essentials Toolkit (see Chapter 3) as a screencasting tool, but I want to share it here, too, in an effort to demonstrate how it can be used in different ways. Jing, at its simplest, gives you the extra boost to make your online communications visual. Jing saves you time and will infuse your online communications with clarity, warmth, and personalization.

Scenarios

Here are two scenarios that show how you can use Jing to enhance communication with your students at a distance.

Scenario #1: Responding to Student Questions with Online Video

Robert Kelley, a psychology professor at MiraCosta College, is in his office responding to emails. He receives a notification that a student has made a post in the "Ask a Question" forum he has set up in his online behavioral statistics class. Robert clicks on the link and is taken to the student's post within his LMS. The student's post reads, "Professor Kelley, I am having difficulty understanding the types of errors regarding hypothesis testing. Can you please explain what the difference between them is?"

As Robert prepares to respond to this question, he has two choices. First, he could type his response, taking extra care to explain his ideas carefully and clearly, perhaps using excerpts from the learning module itself to repeat the ideas for reinforcement. Or, in roughly the same amount of time, he could choose to use Jing to create a video reply, enabling the student to both see and hear the response. With Jing and a microphone, Robert can use his computer screen as a whiteboard to answer his student's questions. Not only will he be able to walk his student through a response but also infuse his teaching with an encouraging, understanding tone.

He chooses to use Jing, and his workflow is simple. To get started, he opens up a blank document in skrbl.com (an online collaborative whiteboard application) or MS Paint and uses it as a whiteboard to illustrate the concept to the student. When he's ready to start his demonstration, he moves his cursor and grabs the crosshair icon from the Jing sun icon hovering in the corner of his screen. He quickly drags the crosshairs across the portion of his screen he wants to record, clicks the "record video" option, waits for the 3–2–1 countdown, and begins to speak. Making sure his explanation is less than five minutes (the max recording time for Jing), he finishes the recording and then clicks "stop." Next, he selects from the two upload options presented to him in Jing: upload to Screencast.com or download to his computer. Robert selects the first option, and within a few minutes, Jing responds, indicating that the URL to his video has been pasted to his computer's clipboard.

Now Robert returns to the student's question and writes, "That is a great question. I have provided you with a video response. You can view it at http:// . . ." By using Jing, Robert has effectively responded to the student's question in a highly personalized way. The student has not only had his question answered but also had a custom video explanation recorded for him. By listening to his professor's explanation, he feels more connected to the material, the class itself, and has another instructional method available to him to learn the material and meet the course objectives. In addition to this, by sharing the instructional Jing video in the discussion forum, Robert has effectively made it available to all other students who may have the same question.

Scenario #2: Providing Voice Feedback on Essays with Jing

Dan Barnett is a philosophy professor at Butte College. As an online instructor, he wants students not only to understand the strengths and weaknesses of their arguments but also to improve their overall writing skills. He makes a great effort to share constructive feedback with students, but he is intimately aware of the amount of time it takes to give each paper a thorough review. Dan wonders if there's a better way to deliver that feedback to his online students. What if he could deliver it with his voice rather than text on a screen? Could Jing be used to humanize the grading experience for students? And if so, how would they respond?

So he tries a new approach in his online Methods of Argument class. Using a CMS with in-line annotation tools, he highlights key areas of a student's paper he would like to discuss.

The goal (since Jing limits videos to five minutes) is to avoid minutiae. Instead, Dan identifies the top-three or so biggest issues the student needs to address. The student may need help with paraphrasing, in how best to write about a philosophical essay, or with an understanding of a central concept.

When he has in mind the areas to discuss, he opens the Jing app, adjusts the crosshairs over the highlighted paper on the screen, clicks "record video," waits for the 3–2–1 countdown, and then speaks directly to the student using the highlights as a guide.

He maintains a steady, helpful tone (even when showing a student that a certain sentence is copied right from the philosopher without attribution) and is careful never to be accusatory or to mention a grade. (The grade for the paper becomes clearer in his mind once he's talked about it, so he enters the grade after recording his comments.)

When he's done, he clicks "stop" and then opts to upload the video to Screencast.com. Jing promptly produces a unique URL for the video, copies it to his computer's clipboard, and then Dan pastes the link into the feedback area for the assignment within the secure gradebook of his CMS. He continues this process until all the papers are graded.

Cynthia, one of Dan's students, logs into the CMS, views her letter grade, clicks the link in the "feedback" area, and views the five-minute video. Hearing her instructor's voice adds a human element to her experience. She really understands where he is coming from and how she can improve her writing, and she doesn't have hurt feelings as she frequently experiences with written feedback.

The screencast.com site tracks views, so Dan is able to see that most students viewed the comments. One student shared the following:

> Even if something comes across as sounding a bit harsh, hearing it in your . . . soothing voice, softens the words and it sounds gentle and encouraging. I am an extremely sensitive person and I get my feelings hurt easily. I love to write and have done very well in other writing classes but have found this class very difficult, so any criticism is difficult for me, even though I know I need it to succeed.

It's important, Dan says, to use video sparingly, and it's true that students needing the most help are least likely to watch (so the use of emerging technologies is not magic). Students are motivated, though, if they know the instructor is keeping notes on the three issues identified and will refer to them in grading subsequent papers.

Finally, it's a good idea to check with your institution regarding student privacy policies before delivering student feedback via a link generated through a third-party tool (even without a grade). These policies can vary greatly from college to college.

 **TIP!**

Use a Skype "Contact Me" Button to Make Yourself Accessible to Students

Skype, a web and mobile app that provides live voice, video, and chat communication, is not featured as an emerging technology in this collection, as it is used quite widely. However, one feature of Skype that isn't well known, but is very useful to instructors, is the Skype "Contact Me" button. It's typical for instructors to include their email address and phone number on a syllabus, but how much more supported would your students be with the ability to click a button in your course site and call or chat with you instantly? Most LMSs have lagged in incorporating these types of rich, instant communication features, but if you want it, Skype delivers it! Essentially, when a student clicks on your customized "Contact Me" button, she is prompted to log into her Skype account and it then be able to see if you are online or not, and initiate a call (or chat) instantly if you appear to be available. This direct form of contact, however, will require you to set your Skype privacy setting to allow "anyone" (that is not just your contacts) to call you. Here's how to create and install your own Skype "Contact Me" button.

1. Go to Skype.com/en/developer/create-contactme-buttons/.
2. Enter your Skype Name in the designated box.
3. Choose what you want your button to do: Call (start a call with a click) or Chat (start a conversation with an instant message).

4.   Choose how you want your button to look (color and size).
5.   Preview the appearance of your button.
6.   Copy the html code that appears in the box.
7.   Go to an area in your course site or LMS (or a web-based syllabus!) where you can access the html code. View and paste the entire string of code. Typically, the html code may be accessed by clicking an icon in a rich text editor's toolbar that looks like this < >, or is labeled "Text View" or "HTML Source."
8.   Click save and your beautiful new button should appear!
9.   Important! In the Privacy area of your Skype preferences, locate the "allow calls from" option and select "anyone" from the drop-down menu.

Animoto—Sleek, Hip Videos Created from Images, Text, Video, and Audio

     Animoto.com/education/classroom—Use this link to request a free Plus account!

Feature Overview

- Easy-to-use, online, or mobile video creation tool.
- Educators can request a free Plus account, which provides unlimited song-length videos without an Animoto watermark for up to one year and a code for up to 50 students to sign up for their own free Plus accounts.
- Free mobile app for iOS and Android, which supports video creation on the go.
- Videos may be shared with a link, embedded on course site, uploaded directly to YouTube, or downloaded to your computer.
- Create videos from still images and 10-second video clips.
- A library of royalty-free images, video clips, and songs are provided at no cost.

Animoto is a super, easy-to-use web-based tool that will make you look like a video editing pro! Once you create your first Animoto video, you'll quickly see the influence of the company's co-founder and ex-MTV producer, Jason Hsiao. After you've created several videos of your family and friends (which you *will do* because it's that fun!), you'll start to see the possibilities Animoto opens for your classes.

Animoto has a simple step-by-step interface that walks you through creating a video using images, video, and audio files saved to your computer; retrieved from the Animoto media library; or from several of your own online accounts (Facebook, Instagram, Dropbox, Flickr, and more). You can easily reorder the media in the creation canvas and add blank slides to which you add your own text. Then select the music for your video from Animoto's royalty-free library, organized by genre with lots to choose from, or your own .mp3 file (if you upload a music file, you must be the song's copyright owner).

Then sit back and relax while Animoto mixes a super hip masterpiece for you! When your video is done, you'll receive an email with a link. The video, now hosted at Animoto.com, can be shared to Facebook, YouTube, and embedded on a website or in a CMS, and you have the option to download a high-res, DVD-quality copy for a nominal fee.

I have used Animoto to create lively video "bumpers" for my classes. I enjoy sharing them with my students for a high-energy start to the semester. You may view one example here: youtu.be/mA1IALdP-tY.

I have also used Animoto to recognize and award significant student achievement. During a semester-long blogging project, I invite students to nominate two peers who have demonstrated "blogging excellence" throughout the semester. I secretly collect the nominations and announce the winner(s) who are rewarded with extra-credit points. I have used Animoto to mix in screenshots from the student blogs and to showcase the work of the award recipients in a special video presentation. View the video here: youtu.be/-N27AfQKYDE.

Anna Stirling, a faculty member at Mt. San Jacinto College, has her students create 30-second Animoto videos in her Introduction to Microsoft Excel class. After a three-week module, the students were instructed to create a "promo" video of Excel to market it to other students. The students were challenged to visually communicate the most important features of Excel using screenshots, as well as images, to symbolically represent their messages. The students posted a link to their videos in a discussion forum and engaged in a dialogue about others' solutions to the problem.

HaikuDeck.com—Beautiful Online Presentations (with Built-In Image Attribution)

Feature Overview

- Free accounts are available but only allow for the creation of three decks, which must be made publicly visible.
- Education accounts are available for a fee with bulk pricing options for departments and entire campuses. Education accounts include the option to
  - create private decks
  - insert playable YouTube videos
  - download decks into PowerPoint format for offline viewing
  - upload a PowerPoint file and have it be automatically transformed into a Haiku Deck

If you are tired of the look and feel of PowerPoint and want to create beautiful, visually centric presentations without the hassle of searching for images with proper licensing options, downloading them, and then uploading them into a separate presentation, Haiku Deck is for you. Haiku Deck presents a user with a simple interface; however, your slide layout options are restricted. Click the thumbnail of the slide layout you prefer, customize the text areas, and without leaving Haiku Deck, search for the right image for your slide. Haiku Deck integrates directly with Flickr and provides you with images that are shared with a CC license. You also have the option to upload your own images into Haiku Deck. When you find the image you want to use on your slide, click it and it is automatically is added to your slide layout. When you are viewing a Haiku Deck, you can view each image's attribution information by clicking the CC icon (top-left corner on the web app and lower-right corner on mobile app). If you export your Haiku Deck to PowerPoint format, the attribution appears on the bottom of each slide.

Figure 4.2 A slide created with Haiku Deck. Photograph by muha, CC-BY. Shared with permission from Haiku Deck.

TIP!

Consider having your students use Haiku Deck to tell a visual story about a topic. Or give them keywords and challenge them to design slides with an image that illustrates each word. This type of visual assessment challenges students to demonstrate knowledge of the meaning of a word and assesses their knowledge in a non-traditional, but engaging, way. Alternatively, have students create a Haiku Deck about themselves as a way to introduce themselves to each other or collect a single photo of each student and create a deck that functions as a course directory.

For more ideas, check out the Pinterest board of Haiku Deck Education Case Studies: Pinterest.com/haikudeck/education-case-studies/.

Adobe Spark—Create Compelling Visual Stories

      Spark.Adobe.com

Feature Overview

- A suite of three free tools: Spark Post (social graphics), Spark Page (single-page websites), Spark Video (animations consisting of images, your voice narration, and music).
- All three tools support the creation of visual stories from your computer or iOS device.
- From within the tools, you may search for CC-licensed images, add them to your project, and the attribution is added for you.

The features of Spark that set it apart from other tools is its ability to support the creation of beautiful content from anywhere (mobile or web) without the need to be a design expert. Adobe touts Spark as a suite of storytelling tools, which make it a perfect option for creating engaging, real-world assessments for your classes. Adobe Post was discussed in Chapter 3. Next, we will dig into Spark Post and Spark Video.

Spark Post

Spark.Adobe.com/about/post

Adobe Spark is a free suite of three easy-to-use tools: Post, Page, and Video. With Post, create single-image graphics with text overlay in minutes. You know those cool graphics you see shared on Facebook and Twitter that include a photograph with an overlay of an inspirational quote? Make your own on your smartphone or computer in moments with Adobe Spark Post. The app also supports the use of video for the background that appears behind the text, which is creates a beautiful effect (envision the sun rising behind your favorite Ralph Waldo Emerson quote). The app provides you with beautiful templates you can manipulate (change the photo, font, colors, sizes, etc.), and as you make changes, the rest of your design will also magically adapt to compliment your edit. When you're done, simply download your file or share it directly to social media networks.

Account Details:

Adobe Spark Post requires you to create an account, but it is free. All of your final designs will be imprinted #AdobeSpark in the corner. With Post, create single-image graphics with text overlay in minutes (see Figure 4.3 for an example).

Spark Page

Spark.Adobe.com/about/page

Turn your words into a stunning, mobile-friendly web page integrated with engaging visuals. Spark Page is an example of a micropublishing tool. It is

Figure 4.3 A graphic I created with Adobe Spark Post and shared on social media to promote a presentation about digital media.

designed to facilitate the quick creation of one-page websites that can be easily shared. The steps are simple:

- Select a theme to set the look and feel of your page.
- Click on the text box to add your own title and select a background image that is used as the background for the title area.
- Click the "plus" icon to add a new block.
- Indicate what type of block you want to add—photo, text, link, video, photogrid (collage), or glideshow (like a slideshow feature).
- Customize the block by adding content to it—add a new block.
- Continue adding content blocks until your page is done.

When your page is complete, click Share and choose your share method: you may copy the shareable link; share to Facebook, Twitter, or email; or copy the embed code. The finished page will show your profile picture and name at the bottom (you may choose to disable these items too), a list of the attributions for the images you've used in the design of your page, and a "made with Adobe Spark Page" tagline (which you cannot remove). At the time of writing, it is possible to embed a Spark Page in an LMS or other web page; however, only the first block of your page will appear in the embedded version. Users will need to click on the block to open your complete Spark Page in a new window.

Spark Video

Spark.Adobe.com/about/video

If you have seen the potential of using video as a form of assessment, but haven't been able to figure out a simple workflow that students of all technology skill levels could manage, you may really enjoy Spark Video. A Spark Video is simple. It's like a slideshow of images (which may be photographs or icons chosen from the search options within the tool or media you pull from your online accounts or hard drive) synced to the your voice. When you start a new video project, you are provided with a series of "story templates" (much like your first step in Spark Post and Page). Your next steps are to record your voice (tell your story); add photos, icons, and text to slides; play it back; and share it. As you work on your video, the tool provides you with a helpful creation framework, which is communicated in the spirit of the theme you chose. For example, if you select the theme titled "A Hero's Journey," you'll be provided with the suggestion to develop five parts to your story: 1) setup, 2) call the adventure, 3) challenge, 4) climax, and 5) resolution. You can certainly veer from this path; however, these bread crumbs keep you aware of your audience. The prompts remind you to be thinking about where you are going with your ideas, as opposed to just speaking and adding images.

You record your story in snippets (just the words you want to play for the current slide you are designing, for example), but you may re-record as many times as you want for each slide. I find recording in this way is much less intimidating than attempting to record an entire story without messing up. I've created videos in under an hour on my computer in my office using a USB headset microphone and on my iPad sitting on a comfy chair in my living room sipping red wine. The mobile experience (even without the wine) is quite nice. Just be cautious of background noise while recording.

Here is an example of a "story" I created with Adobe Video, which I also used as a promotion for this book! Spark.Adobe.com/video/rJn-GCCv

Populr—Single-Page, Mobile-Friendly Websites with Varied Layouts

Populr.me

Feature Overview

- Free accounts with premium options.
- Drag and drop editing.
- Templates for education provide a helpful starting point.
- Clone features allows you to share your page with others as a template.
- Option to point your pages to your custom domain (you must have a domain registered already).

Populr is a micropublishing tool (like Adobe Spark Page). It is a multifunctional tool that can be used to create a detailed online promotion for an event, an assignment overview, an online resource list for students to reference during a class, a site to provide to your presentation audience with an embedded version of your slides, related links, and your photo and contact info, or a digital syllabus containing a friendly welcome video and engaging graphics (see the showcase that follows). If you use an LMS for your class content, but would like to have a simple way to create online web pages that students can access without needing to stumble through the tricky log-in process, this might be your solution.

Populr offers a variety of themes to choose from, which you may customize with your own background image, font, and font color. You may also start your page using one of the tool's templates, which include options for education (faculty listing, course page, syllabus, class project, announcements, and more). What sets it apart from Adobe Page, however, is its support of complex layouts. Adobe Page allows only a single block or column for each row, which is limiting. With Populr, you can create complex magazine-like layouts: a single-column row at the top for a title, a double-column row for your name/title and photo, a three-column row for a mix of text and image, etc. Building the website itself is as simple as dragging a new content block into a row. As you work with Populr, you will find that adding multiple content blocks into a single row can improve the appearance of your media. For example, if an image is the only block in a row, the image will be sized to fill the entire width of the page. That usually doesn't look so great. The only way to scale down the image is to add additional blocks to that row. This process takes some time to get used to.

A process I find helpful is to use a Populr page of my own as a template to get myself started more quickly with a new one. You can do this easily from the "My Pages" area of your account by clicking the arrow next to the title of the page you want to copy and selecting "duplicate" from the drop-down menu. Alternatively, you can also transform one of your pages into a template by using the "clone" link (follow the aforementioned steps, but select "Collaborate" from the drop-down menu, click the box next to "Enable Clone Link," and click "copy link"). If a person clicks on your clone link, she is prompted to log into her Populr account and then an editable version of the page appears on the screen. This is a second version of your site, which means the changes that are made to it do not interfere with your own page. Clone links can be very useful if you are having students create projects in Populr. For example, you could create a template for a project that students populate with necessary content, in accordance with your rubric. Starting students off with a template improves their understanding of your expectations.

 TIP!

Create a Liquid Syllabus

Your syllabus is important, right? You put a lot of time into it, and you expect students to use it and refer back to it. But how mobile-friendly is your syllabus? Does it require students to log into an LMS to access it? How reader-friendly is it? And does it convey a sense of who you are? You may not think that's important for a syllabus to do, but remember reading your syllabus is often a student's first experience in your class.

Using a micropublishing tool like Populr to create a liquid syllabus is a game changer. Moving away from a print-based syllabus empowers you to incorporate a warm welcome video, inviting images related to your course content, and integrate links, allowing for multi-layered content that presents the critical information on the top layer with the option to click to read more.

Several years ago, while teaching History of Photography online, I made the change to a liquid syllabus created with Populr. I began referring to it as my "humanized syllabus," because I took such pride in sharing it with students and colleagues. I really felt connected to it and began to put a great deal of work into ensuring it was a positive "experience" for my students, as opposed to thinking of it as a list of policies, materials, and course details. I felt present in my syllabus. I also embedded a lively course bumper video that I had created with Animoto, screenshots of our digital assignments (VoiceThreads and blogs), and a PDF version of the syllabus at the end for anyone who needed or wanted it. If you'd like to view a sample of my syllabus or make a clone of it, follow the links provided!

View syllabus: Brocansky.Populr.me/liquid-syllabus
Clone syllabus: Populr.me/clone/57916427a956aaa9fe000025/pknwqhsezb4e302 pcddg6mnj

Summary

This chapter has provided you with a collection of emerging tools that can be used to enhance your communications and the sharing of content with your students. The set of tools discussed in this chapter by no means includes all of your options, but such tools are offered to inspire you to see the possibilities of moving your online communications and content beyond the realm of text. Audio, video, images, and mobile devices are the 21st-century palette from which you are invited to craft your own masterful teaching and learning experience. When students sit in front of a computer to learn, they will be more engaged and motivated week after week in a long semester journey when they can see you, hear you, and have options to learn from anywhere.

In the next chapter, you will explore more tools that open up an array of possibilities for participatory learning and student-generated content—the next step in transforming your teaching through emerging technologies.

Notes

1. Brown, B. (2015). *How the Course to Be Vulnerable Transforms the Way We Live, Love, Parent, and Lead.* New York, NY: Gotham Books, 2012.
2. Pacansky-Brock, M. (2016). Humanizing Online Learning. *SlideShare.* Retrieved on July 16, 2016 from www.slideshare.net/brocansky/humanizing-online-learning-60892828.

Chapter 5

Tools for Participatory Learning

Twitter? Really?

In 2008, when Twitter was becoming a household word, I resisted using it—with passion. I was already feeling over-committed to the number of social networks I had joined and was feeling excited about many new tools I was using. For the life of me, I could not justify why I would want to use a tool that was going to spit out up to 140-character message updates about what people were doing. Really? Me a "tweeter?" What was I going to do? Follow Justin Timberlake? I had written Twitter off as an annoying, immature, superficial nuisance that clearly would add no value to my existence.

Then I found myself sitting at a conference with the complex, multi-colored session brochure laid out in front of me. I was intensely analyzing the sessions, narrowing them down by circling the ones I thought looked best—always finding more than one at each time that I wanted to go to. As I was doing this, the presenter of the general session was informing participants about the Twitter "hashtag" for the conference. I felt stupid because, while I had heard of Twitter, I had no clue what on earth a "hashtag" was and she didn't clarify. I guess that was the moment I felt like I was being left behind (a feeling I don't like much when it comes to new technologies) but also a little intrigued. Here I was at a conference for higher education focused on emerging technologies and Twitter was integrated front and center. I could feel myself trying to avoid it but deep down I knew I was going to have to give Twitter a try.

Reluctantly, I set up my Twitter account and made my first tweet, revealing my aversion, "Here it goes—another social networking tool. Could it be time for therapy?" Like most social technologies, Twitter didn't feel social immediately. The early stages of using a new tool involves the cultivation of your community, which includes the users you want to follow and those who follow you. That part took a while.

So I set out to decode the "hashtag" concept that had been referenced earlier in the day. I was on to something when I noticed that while I was sending my tweets from my account on Twitter.com, there was a neat little stream of tweets appearing in a time line feed on the conference website—packaged nicely into a little vertical box. The conference's hashtag time line was created using a Twitter search widget. Each time a conference participant sent a tweet that included the conference hashtag, the tweet appeared in the feed. A widget, again, is like a miniaturized and sometimes customized version of an application that can be embedded on a website or in a LMS (see Chapter 1 for details on embedding).

 **TIP!**

Hashtag How-To

A hashtag is, simply, a word or group of characters preceded by the hash (or number) sign, #. Hashtags may not include spaces, commas, periods, exclamation points, question marks, or apostrophes. They are useful, as they allow users to tag their social media content with words or phrases that allow other users to locate, collect, and follow real-time conversations about specific topics.

Hashtags are not limited to Twitter, however. All media tools, including Instagram, Facebook, Google+, Tumblr, and Pinterest, support them. For example, if I make a post on Instagram (and I have my account settings adjusted to "public") and include a particular hashtag and you make a post on Facebook that includes that same hashtag (with your post settings adjusted to "public"), anyone may go to Google.com (or any other web search tool), enter the hashtag into the search box, click enter, and view our content alongside all other publicly visible content shared with the hashtag. Keep in mind that web search results are not instant. Online content must be indexed prior to it appearing in search results. Alternatively, if you are using a social media tool, the hashtag itself appears as hyperlink within your content. Clicking on it will display a stream of all recent content shared with that tool that includes that particular hashtag.

Grasping the concept of an embedded Twitter time line (which, by the way, used to be referred to as a Twitter widget) was a big step in understanding how a user, like me, could locate, extract, and organize information relevant to my needs from the messy, matted, and unappealing ball of hair that I imagined Twitter to be. Now I was beginning to see the pesky little tool as a powerful grassroots communication tool, and I felt intrigued to be part of the conversation.

Over the next two days at the conference, I used Twitter and the hashtag to share my own thoughts and reflections about the sessions I attended and deeper connections I was making. That was great, but what was really exciting, for me, was how the Twitter feed allowed me to read the fleeting thoughts of those attending a session two doors down, which I would, otherwise, be completely unable to access. There was actually more than one time when I chose to leave one session and join another because I could tell from the tweets that it was more relevant to my own needs. I also found it rather interesting (and still do) when I find myself sitting in a room reading the tweets of other people in the room with me. I find myself peering around trying to find out who is saying what—often because I think their ideas are intriguing and I want to hear more!

Since my entry into the Twitterverse in 2008, I've also had many opportunities to engage in conference backchannels that I couldn't attend in person. As I sit at home in my office, I can read the tweets of those I follow who are at a conference on the other side of the country. This is always fun and offers an opportunity to glean resources and engage in some dialogue with educators who are physically present at the event. Walls are no longer barriers in a participatory society. In fact, now when I jump into a conference backchannel and recognize a user's name, I almost always respond with, "Are you here?" Attending face-to-face conferences has become an exciting opportunity for me to meet the individuals I follow on Twitter and who regularly contribute to my lifelong learning.

 TIP!

Get Connected with Twitter Hashtags

Getting familiar with commonly used Twitter hashtags is a helpful way for you to find information relevant to your interests. Enter any hashtag into the "search" box on Twitter.com and you'll retrieve a time line of all the most recent tweets sent with that hashtag.

If you'd like to designate a hashtag for your own class, college campus, or department, all you have to do is determine the precise group of characters you'd like to use. It's a good idea to plug it into the Twitter search box to be sure it's not a popular one already—that is, unless contributions from the Twitter community might improve your dialogue. Also keep in mind that hashtags are not like URLs. You cannot "own" one. There's always a chance another group may begin to use it, so shoot for something unique if exclusivity is important to you.

If you're building your Twitter network and looking to engage in some education-related chat, here are a few popular hashtags you may want to try out.

- **#onlinelearning**—chat about online learning
- **#edtech**—Tweets related to technology in education
- **#highered**—news related to college and universities
- **#comm_college**—news related to community colleges
- **#flipclass**—resources related to the flipped classroom model (see Introduction)
- **#accessibility**—supporting the needs of individuals with disabilities
- **#elearning**—web-enhanced or online learning

As you start following users on Twitter, take note of who provides you with great ideas (these may include comments, quotes, or links to articles, tools, and/or blog posts). Click on a user's name to go to the user's profile, where you will see the time line of tweets sent from that account. Along the top of the time line, you may have the option to learn more about the user. Click on "Following" to see who the user follows, "Followers" to see who follows that user, "Likes" to see a time line of tweets that user has liked, and "Lists" to see a list of publicly viewable lists that user has been added to.

SHOWCASE

Follow Fifty—Teaching Students to Harness Twitter

Catherine Hillman, who teaches Social Media for Marketing at Cuesta College, gives her students an activity that requires them to use Twitter to locate and follow fifty experts in a topic related to their interests. The activity engages students with Twitter as a learning resource and facilitates a meaningful relationship with social media that extends well beyond the superficial application social media tools typically play in the lives of students. Through the activity, students learn how to mine Twitter for relevant content and evaluate the tweets in their time line using a process that Hillman refers to as "Signal-to-Noise" ratio: determine whose posts provide relevant information for your interests ("Signal") and eliminate those whose posts are not relevant to you ("Noise"). To view the lesson plan for Hillman's "Follow Fifty" activity (shared with a CC license) refer to the Chapter 5 online resources at TeachingWithEmergingTech.com.

The Backchannel: Teaching in a Participatory Classroom

Trying to get more students to participate is a common struggle for college professors. "No matter what I do, it's always the same students who raise their hands." Sound familiar? Well, be careful what you wish for! The grassroots nature of social media is making some sweeping changes in how, when, and where people participate.

With a smartphone, tablet, or laptop connected to Twitter, learning from and with people anywhere in the world is literally just a few clicks away. According to Twitter, in March 2016, the company had more than 320 million monthly active users, and it supports 40 languages. Roughly 83% of actively users access Twitter with a mobile device, and 79% are outside the United States.[1] In 2015, in the United States, about 23% of online adults used Twitter, which was a 6% growth from 2013.[2]

In 2011, during the rise in Twitter's popularity, the world witnessed an empowering effect of social media as Egyptians shared their experiences with the world via Twitter from the street corners of Cairo. Mobile technology and social media assisted Egyptian revolutionaries with organizing and sharing their experiences, reactions, and dreams about the future with the world in real time with text, pictures, and video.

The impact that Mubarak's resignation announcement on February 11, 2011, had on the Twitterverse was captured by André Panisson with a cutting-edge visualization technology (see Figure 5.1) as part of an international research

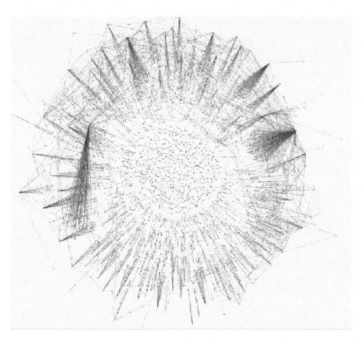

Figure 5.1 Twitter visualization. Printed with permission from André Panisson with credit to the Computer Science Department of the University of Turin and the ISI Foundation in Turin.

study. The video (which can be viewed on YouTube at youtu.be/2guKJfvq4uI) translates each tweet sent with the hashtag #Jan25, which became synonymous with messages referencing events of the revolution, into a tiny node, and as each tweet is "retweeted" (forwarded by a user onto his/her own network), the node blossoms into a burst of more nodes. The video is fascinating to watch, as it illustrates the speed at which information can travel around the world with a mobile, social media tool such as Twitter, but it also offers each of us an opportunity to see a visual representation of what participatory learning looks like.

Twitter flattens the playing field by distributing power to all and giving members of the community the opportunity to hold each user accountable for his or her actions. Introducing Twitter into the classroom rocks the foundations of "the lecture," as a "presentation" is no longer linear, and the flow of questions and comments are no longer controllable by a single authoritative figure. Again, this is why we began with a focus on "community" and "community groundrules" in Chapter 1.

The phone in a person's hand is a symbol of our new participatory society. Multimedia content creation and global engagement are now in our pockets. Feature phones—a term that simply refers to a mobile phone without an Internet connection—and smartphones both have the capability to send and receive tweets (which may be written messages, snapshots, or, in more and more instances, videos). Feature phones can be easily connected to a user's Twitter account using SMS text messaging. What this means to you is that your students' fleeting ideas and questions that used to be silent and unobtrusive now bubble to the surface when phones are used as learning tools in a classroom. The result is a "backchannel." And, as many people are discovering at conferences as well as in the classroom, that backchannel can occur with or without your acknowledgment.

Cliff Atkinson, author of *The Backchannel: How Audiences are Using Twitter and Social Media and Changing Presentations Forever*, defines a backchannel as

> a line of communication created by people in an audience to connect with others inside or outside the room, with or without the knowledge of the speaker at the front of the room. Usually facilitated by Internet technologies, it is spontaneous, self-directed, and limited in time to the duration of a live event.[3]

Backchannels are not specific to Twitter usage, but they are a phenomenon that has been influenced through the popularization of social media and the use of mobile devices. While the idea of a backchannel may make you uncomfortable and even offer one more reason to ban cell phones from your classroom, some professors think they hold opportunities for improving classroom learning.

Backchannels are now mainstream. When we watch a live event on television, we are offered a hashtag to use to contribute our own thoughts or to view the thoughts of others. Often samples of viewers' tweets appear along the bottom of our screen, presenting us with the ability to view the event through the lenses of multiple individuals, in addition to our own. With a backchannel, an experience that was once passive is now interactive. This new multidimensional experience adds fascinating opportunities for educators to engage students in a complex fabric of multi-layered viewpoints and amplify the voices of all students.

Social technologies, such as Twitter, have paved the way for the emergence of cloud-based Student Response Software (SRS), which has replaced Clicker Response Systems (or clickers) that had previously been popular in higher education. With a focus on increasing engagement, SRS tools (such as PollEverywhere and Top Hat, which are both discussed later in this chapter) empower students to turn a passive lecture experience into an interactive journey. While clickers required students to have access to a particular device that would grant them the ability to contribute a response to a question posed by their instructor, SRS eliminates the need for the additional device. When instructors use an SRS, students may make contributions during class (or after) by using an app installed on their smartphones or tablets or by going directly to a designated link on their laptops. SRS tools leverage the participatory spirit of a "backchannel," but provide instructors with more opportunities to align student contributions with instructional content.

Derek Bruff, a senior lecturer and director of the Center for Teaching at Vanderbilt University and author of *Teaching with Classroom Response System: Creating Active Learning Environments*, theorizes that backchannel tools offer opportunities to enhance the type of student engagement clickers initiate. He considers participating in a backchannel as a form of "active listening." Drawing from his own experiences, Bruff reflects,

> When I attend a keynote talk at a conference, I'll often tweet about the most interesting points made by the speaker, and I'll sometimes respond to comments made about the talk by others on the backchannel. That's not some form of distraction or even multitasking—it's active listening. I think it's great that teachers are encouraging students to listen actively in similar ways in the classroom.[4]

Some professors, such as Bruff, are stepping out to test the waters of back-channels and explore how this new social terrain can be used to support, rather than derail, learning. From my experiences, what these professors have in common is an interest in increasing student participation in a class (physical or online) and an awareness of student learning differences. Many students feel completely comfortable asking questions in a lecture setting, but this isn't typical of *all* students. Other students, perhaps most, will never speak up—out of fear of sounding stupid, feeling inadequate (maybe the student feels badly about her accent or was responded to in a poor manner by a professor in another class), or as a result of a cognitive learning disorder that simply affects the pace and rhythm of his learning. These are the students who are more likely to tune out and who are challenged by the traditional lecture environment. Backchannel tools can provide more options for students to participate, as opposed to acting as a replacement for the verbal dialogue in a class.

SHOWCASES

The Twitter Experiment (In-Class Use)

Dr. Monica Rankin, professor of history at UT Dallas, was an early adopter of Twitter in the classroom for a backchannel tool. Her work is showcased in a brief and informative video on YouTube titled "The Twitter Experiment" (youtu.be/6WPVWDkF7U8), which was produced by Kim Smith, a grad student in Emerging Media and Communications at UT Dallas. With help from her TA, Megan Malone, Rankin established a Twitter hashtag and encouraged her students to use their laptop or cell phone to send tweets. Rankin's 90-student class met three times each week: twice for a lecture and once, on Fridays, for a quiz and discussion. The use of Twitter was encouraged after the quiz each Friday.

Rankin notes that she had many students who didn't know what Twitter was and had to set up accounts. Despite being encouraged to do so before class, most waited until class time to take care of that step. The first two weeks of Twitter activity was mostly "start-up" content ("Test, test"; "How does this work?"; etc.) with a few meaningful tweets. This is an important point, as there is always a "start-up" period with using new technologies in a class, and I think instructors who understand this will plan for it rather than view it as a nuisance, and they will be more successful with their instructional goals.

Rankin acknowledges that her experiment required her to reassess things week by week and to try new things. She found that the tweets became more insightful, and the in-class discussions became more dynamic when students were placed into small groups of three to five and given a topic to discuss (verbally). The groups were instructed to identify the "best" ideas and tweet them for the rest of the class to engage their contributions.

Throughout the discussions, the Twitter stream with the students' contributions (with use of a Twitter "search widget") was projected on a large screen in front of the class, and students with Internet access could open it and view it on their own laptops or smartphones. Rankin also observed that, like most small group activities, the quality increased the more she and her TA circulated around the classroom and checked in with groups to facilitate their ideas.

Malone, Rankin's TA, noted that the experiment was exciting, because typically in a discussion, there are only three to four students who willingly participate, and with Twitter, this number increased tenfold. Additionally, having the tweets available online enabled her to go back and follow up with the students' tweets over the weekend with the option to send them a "direct message" (or DM) which is a private exchange on Twitter. Bobby Sibert, a student featured in Rankin's video, points out that the tweets shared by his classmates became a valuable study resource after class as well.

There were challenges, of course, including the 140-word limitation imposed on each tweet. But Rankin realizes that Twitter isn't the best tool for discussion of complex ideas; rather, it should be theorized as a tool that students can use *when* they have an idea or question appropriate for a tweet, as opposed to when it's appropriate to engage in a verbal conversation with their class peers. Moreover, she observes that requiring students to limit their ideas to 140 characters forces the students to filter their ideas and to think about what they want to say and how to best say it in a succinct way. Twitter forcing students to focus? Hm. That's an interesting twist.

Rankin also accommodated students who didn't have a smartphone or laptop by allowing them to hand write their comments and give them to the TA, who would post them to the feed after class was over. Additionally, in one instance, she engaged the Twitter stream of student comments while she was out of state traveling at a conference. As her TA conducted the discussion in person, Rankin chimed in on the feed, "Your instructor is present," and participated virtually in the exchanges. Again, walls are no longer barriers to participation!

Twitter Hashtags Beyond the Walls of a Classroom

Dr. Diane Gusa teaches Pedagogy and Technology of Online Learning at SUNY Canton. In this online course, she immerses her students in the use of Twitter to learn how it can foster teaching presence and students' social presence, as well as build one's professional learning network (PLN)—powerful outcomes for future online educators! To do this, Dr. Gusa designates a course hashtag (#EDUC300), provides the hashtag to her students, and instructs the students to send tweets about their learning that include the hashtag. Dr. Gusa participates with her students, regularly tweeting from her account with the hashtag.

At the start of the term, students in Gusa's class are not entirely on board with this plan. There is little buy-in about how brief tweets can help students feel connected to one another. Gusa is aware of this reluctance and does her best to support and encourage students through the early stages of the class. Her own participation on Twitter models the effective use of Twitter to her students. Heavy modeling in the early stages of an online class is essential to on-boarding new, reluctant students. In a final blog post, one of Gusa's students shared,

> *"If you asked me at the beginning of this course if I believed (developing teaching presence and social presence) could be done by utilizing social media, I would have told you, "No way."... I have seen the light and am amazed at how much Twitter enhanced this course and broadened my horizons. It fostered our EDUC 300 learning community as we*

encouraged, motivated and helped each other out. Often times I felt like I was getting one-on-one guidance in public ..."

When the course ends, the hashtag still has a function to former students. As long as they continue to use Twitter, the past students will have continued access to the hashtag conversations that ensue between students in Gusa's future classes. This provides an ongoing process for keeping current students connected in a network with past students. After class ends, Gusa transitions from course instructor to member of her students' PLN.

Tools for Participatory Learning Environments

Participatory learning is the form of learning that occurs through interactions in the public web and with social media, such as Twitter, Facebook, and YouTube. Informed by mainstream adoption of social technologies and mobile devices, participatory learning is reshaping the way we learn. Learning is participatory when the outcome is a product that has been constructed through contributions made by members of a group or community.

In *The Future of Thinking*, Cathy Davidson and David Theo Goldberg use participatory learning synonymously with "digital learning" and examine how it challenges many hallmarks of academia.

> With digital learning, the play between technology, composer, and audience is no longer passive . . . In conventional learning institutions, the lines of authorship and authority are clearly delineated, and the place of teacher, student, and technology are well known. With digital learning, these conventional models of authority break down.[5]

Transitioning into a participatory learning environment can be nerve-racking for a professor, as I reflected in the introduction where I share my "flipped classroom" experiment. When you've been positioned as the one with the answers whose responsibility it is to pass information on to students and ensure they *know* it, facilitating a participatory learning environment may make you feel as if the stable ground beneath you is crumbling away. My advice is to remember that your role is still *essential*. It's not any less important, just different.

To understand how I have integrated participatory learning in my own classes, visualize a spectrum with "accessing content" at one end and "contributing content" at the other. If each of my students' learning experiences could be tracked visually on this continuum, the node representing their actions would continually shift from left to right: from accessing to contributing, back to accessing, then again to contributing. In my learning units, students begin by accessing information in a variety of formats (videos, articles, chapters, images, and audio either created by me, provided as part of the course materials, created by the students in a previous unit, or a combination of all three) and then apply what they've learned in participatory learning activities (creating and commenting on blog posts, commenting in and adding slides to a VoiceThread, collaboratively producing Google Slides, etc.).

Each student understands that his/her goal is to master the learning objectives for that particular unit. After a student has accessed the assigned content and made the required contributions, they "access" the contributions made by their peers—looping back to the opposite end of the spectrum—and then leave comments and feedback that loops back again. As students regularly contribute their own content (in response to the activities I have designed) and interact with the student-generated content to deconstruct, discuss, apply, analyze it, the more *participatory* the learning environment is.

The following pages offer a selection of tools that offer potential for participatory learning and several practical examples of how professors are using them to innovate their teaching approaches.

Slack—A Communication Tool for Teams

 Slack.com

Feature Overview

- A social communications tool for invited team members that keeps everyone connected across computers, phones, and tablets.
- Free for the first 10,000 messages and then an upgrade is required.
- Invite team (or class) members using a link.
- Conversations are organized by channels, which define common themes.
- Channels can be public (open to all team members) or private (only select team members may join).
- When links to media (Google Docs, YouTube videos, images, and more) are included in a post, the media is automatically embedded.
- Individual and group direct message feature.
- Search features provides easy way to locate topics.
- Users may program "do not disturb" hours to turn notifications off during non-work times.
- Terrific online support that includes helpful getting started guides.

If you've been looking for a communication tool other than email that is efficient, easy to use, and flexible, you will love Slack. Slack is designed to support internal team communications for the workplace, but can be used to support class interactions (Figure 5.2). The channels feature is a perfect way to organize topics and create private spaces for small groups of students to interact and work on projects. Team members post messages and content directly into specific channels (or create a new channel if an appropriate one does not exist), and, in the process, everything in Slack is indexed and archived in one place, as opposed to separate emails and text messages. Slack becomes like a searchable archive of all your class or team communications and content. Slack connects with more than 500 applications (including Zoom, Google Hangouts, Google Docs, Skype, and Twitter), which streamlines the user experience by creating a single content portal for all your team's tools. One of my favorite features of Slack is the ability to react to any message with an emoji. Team members can quickly share a "thumbs up" icon, for example, to indicate that they are in agreement instead of responding with an additional message.

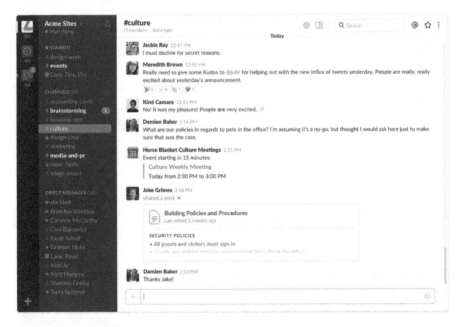

Figure 5.2 Screenshot of team communications in Slack. Used with permission from Slack.

Padlet—Post to a Digital Bulletin Board from a Phone Without an Account

 Padlet.com

Feature Overview

- Free accounts for individuals and premium institutional licenses.
- Padlet is like a digital piece of paper that students can post to without an account from a mobile device or computer.
- Posts may include links, photos (online, uploaded from your computer, or taken from your webcam/phone), and typed responses.
- Privacy options include private, password protected, secret (unlisted), public.
- You choose the access level you want others to have: can read (view only), can write (view and post), can moderate (view, post, edit and approve other posts).
- Embed code makes it easy to put a Padlet in your course.
- Customizable backgrounds.
- Grid or free-flow organization options.
- May be shared with a link or embedded in a website or LMS.

Padlet has many uses! It's a terrific tool to coordinate a brainstorming activity—post names of famous artists—to kick off a new unit, assess engagement by having students post their clearest or muddiest point from a class, or review for a test by proposing exam questions. When you create a Padlet, you have the option to use a custom URL, which makes sharing the link with students in a class much easier. Padlet incorporates a range of privacy options, too, including the option to identify a moderator for your board, and instantly provides a QR code for each Padlet you create. One caveat to be aware of, however, is that the posts on a Padlet are anonymous. You will need to instruct your students to include their names at the top of their posts if you want to be able to identify them.

I've used Padlet in an online course as a place for students to post questions prior to a synchronous meeting. For example, I arrange a live meeting with my students and ask them to post topics on the Padlet board that they'd like us to discuss. This process helps students to understand that our live time together is not a time for me to lecture; rather, it's a time to discuss their questions. I find that students are more willing to list these topics using Padlet than raise the questions during a live session.

Figure 5.3 Screenshot of a Padlet. Used with permission from Padlet.

Would you like to give Padlet a try? Here is a sample I created for you to experiment with (shown in Figure 5.3). Try it out from your phone too: padlet. com/brocansky/tryit.

Tackk

   Tackk.com

Feature Overview

- Free. At the time of writing, Tackk is planning to release a premium account for educators that will improve the ability to collect and review student work.
- Create single-page social websites.
- Public and unlisted publishing options.
- Drag and drop interface enables easy multimedia integration (plug in a URL from YouTube, search for a photo from 500px, upload a graphic of your own, type instructions or a reflection).

- Creative options for customizing the look and feel of your site.
- Instantly collect all of your students' sites by using the Tackboard feature (discussed next).

Tackk provides an easy way to create a single web page with the option to include a stream at the bottom of the page in which others may leave comments. Commenting on a Tackk does not require a person to have an account; however, account holders have the ability to add images and videos to their comments. And the Tackkboard feature is especially appealing to instructors who like the idea of having students use Tackk, but struggle with understanding how to track, view, and assess all the individual links created by students.

 **TIP!**

Create a Tackkboard—A Collection of Tackks with a Consistent Tag

A Tackkboard is a URL that showcases all of the public Tackks that are tagged with the same keyword. The URL for a Tackkboard always follows this logic: tackk.com/board/*tag*. Replace *tag* with the keyword that each Tackk is tagged with. When you create or edit a Tackk, you will find a field labeled Tackkboards in the Options area. This is where you enter the tags. This feature has many applications for teaching and learning. One downside to Tackkboards is the appearance of an ad at the top of the page.

I used Tackk to create a module overview for each module in my History of Still Photography online course. I did this because creating an overview page in Tackk produces more visually appealing content than using the editor in my LMS. In Tackk, I can easily embed an engaging photograph at the top that relates to our module and add a brief YouTube video of myself introducing the unit, select a lively color and pattern, and then I embed the Tackk right inside my LMS (I've done this in Blackboard and Canvas), and it's also available publicly. With the content publicly accessible, I am able to include a link to each module overview in the course syllabus. This way, students always have a clear list of the weekly activities, even before class starts, and they have access to the overviews in the LMS and in the syllabus. I find this helpful for students, as many of them are away for parts of the semester, and the overviews allow them to look ahead and see what we'll be doing during their time away. In my syllabus, I also include a link to the Tackkboard, which is a page students can visit to view all of the overviews in one place. To view all of the module overview Tackks, go to tackk.com/board/hosp.

I have also used Tackk for a student-generated, extra-credit website project. The activity was titled Photo Quest. Students chose one of three challenges and created a Tackk (tagged with the same keyword) as the final deliverable. The challenges (Who am I? and Where do I come from?) required students to engage on a more intimate level with photographs. Students were required to have conversations about their ancestry and family history with family members and/or friends. The conversations had to be accompanied by photographs. The student's goal was to identify one photograph that played a significant role in unveiling a part of his or her past that was unknown. Then, in a Tackk, the student shared a digital version of the photograph and wrote about the experience. In short, the Tackks were like blog posts. One of my students shared a faded image of himself and his sister at ages three and five, each clutching an old toy. He went on to explain that the photograph showed him on his first day of kindergarten in Mexico. His teacher had given every student a toy to take home. At pickup, upon seeing all of the other children with toys, his toyless sister began to cry. His teacher reached out and gave her a toy too. The picture shows them both happy and proudly displaying their toys. My student didn't have a memory of this event before having the conversation about the photograph, and he also did not know that he had attended kindergarten in Mexico.

ThingLink—Make Images Interactive

 ThingLink.com

Feature Overview

- Many account types including Basic Education (free), Pro Teacher (includes a groups feature for managing classes), Premium Teacher (and Schools/Districts).
- Compare account features here: thinglink.com/edu-options.

With ThingLink, you can turn any digital image into an interactive bulletin board. The posts (or "things") that are added to an image in ThingLink unlock an additional layer of information about the visual content. For example, a photograph of a building may reveal hidden architectural terms; a campus map could contain memories from students' freshman semester; an image of a well-known photograph may unveil stories about the photograph's context, photographer's life, or process used to make it; and an old master painting may identify the figures illustrated in the shadows. Break students up into small groups, assign one ThingLink challenge to each group, and see how much information they can add to an image in 10 minutes. Then project each image and review their contributions as a class. Or at the end of a class, post a picture about an important topic that was covered and have students write a two- to three-sentence takeaway about the lesson. This is an engaging way to integrate a formative assessment at the end of class.

TodaysMeet—Temporary Digital Rooms for Backchannels

TodaysMeet.com

Feature Overview

- Free and easy to use.
- Those participating in the conversation do not need an account to comment.
- Upgraded account provides access to these "Teacher Tools": permanent access to room transcripts, ability to pause rooms, limit room membership to students at your institution, password protect rooms, moderate conversations, post a prompt at the top of your room's page to keep conversations focused.

TodaysMeet is simple, easy to use, and multifunctional. It is a great tool to use during a class session or presentation when you want to see a mass response to a particular question or if you want to try out a backchannel but don't want to hassle with a tool like Twitter that not everyone uses. However, the simplicity of TodaysMeet limits the options you have for formatting your questions. Essentially, TodaysMeet is a place where anyone can type open-ended messages in a simple, vertical feed. You cannot create multiple-choice questions; you cannot display responses in a word cloud; you simply have a space with a feed of comments. Which is just perfect for some things!

Only those who you provide the link to will be able to access your Todays-Meet room. And when a person arrives, she will be prompted to give herself a "nickname." That nickname will appear underneath each contribution she makes. When you create a TodaysMeet, you indicate when you want the room to close (that is, disappear). At any time, you may click the save transcript feature and download (or print) a PDF of the entire conversation. There is also a clean presentation view that works well when you are using the tool with a live audience.

Poll Everywhere—Student Response Software with a Free Account Option

    PollEverywhere.com

Feature Overview

- Create polls, questions that students can respond to with text messaging or any Internet-connected device.
- Free and premium accounts. Special pricing available for higher education accounts.
- Free accounts limit each poll to 40 responses.
- With a premium account, you can organize students into groups for competitive quizzes.
- Various question types allow results to be displayed live in many different formats including a live feed and word cloud.
- Download poll results in .CSV format.
- Project polls from the web or insert them into your PowerPoint, Keynote, or Google Slides presentation.

Sandra C. Haynes, an art history professor at Pasadena City College, uses Poll-Everywhere in her large lecture classes. With her free account, she can easily create simple, single-question polls with a multiple-choice or open-ended response and build them into her classroom pedagogy. She often surprises her students with a "beginning of class" poll of 10 or so questions as a formative assessment for material students were supposed to have prepared for that day's class. She may also use polling during the lecture to evaluate student engagement and comprehension. When it's time for a poll, her students know the drill—they whip out a phone, tablet, or laptop to respond to the poll. After a 30-second pause for responses to be collected, the responses are tallied and presented "live" in a visual format on the digital screen for both Haynes and her students to see.

As noted earlier in this chapter, Poll Everywhere is an updated version of a classroom response system (aka "clickers"), but this solution doesn't require the institution to purchase clickers or for the instructor to take time to check them out to students. Rather, students are empowered to use their existing mobile devices as learning tools. And while the 40-person limit for a free Poll Everywhere account sounded like a challenge to me, Haynes responded quite differently, explaining that her students are aware that not every vote will be recorded, so the response limitation actually creates a kind of lively competition within the classroom. Furthermore, in her flipped classroom model, Haynes divides students into teams, with only the team captain responsible for submitting an answer to the poll. Aside from having the opportunity to engage her students and to check in on their learning throughout a lecture, Haynes says she also loves using the tool because it's a great feeling to see students get so excited about being encouraged to use their phones in class!

VoiceThread

 VoiceThread.com

Feature Overview

- New accounts start as free, but require a premium upgrade after five Voice-Threads have been created. Free accounts, however, support unlimited commenting.
- Create *asynchronous* voice and video conversations around media (presentations, images, videos, and more).
- Students may leave comments in voice (with a microphone or phone), video (with a webcam), or text (with a keyboard).
- Upgraded accounts include privacy options: secure, semi-private, and public.
- While commenting, users use their mouse (or finger on the mobile app) to annotate on the media shared in the center of a slide, and when another user plays that comment back, the annotation plays in sync with the user's voice.
- Institutions with a site license have access to the LTI plug-in, which can be integrated with a campus single sign-on, resulting in the auto-creation of faculty and student accounts, gradebook integration, and more.
- Captions can be uploaded for comments and central media. Site license holders can partner with a third-party captioning company to request captions on demand.
- VoiceThread Universal provides support for users who are blind and navigate the web with a screenreader, an assistive technology device.

VoiceThread is a tool that I have used in my classes since 2007. It has become integral to my online teaching and has also played a big role in changing the way I have taught my face-to-face classes too (see the introduction for a reflection of my "flipped classroom" experiment featuring VoiceThread). Teaching with VoiceThread can extend meaningful conversations beyond the walls of a classroom; empower all students to speak; and incorporate your warm, human presence into an online or blended class.

VoiceThread is asynchronous or "time shifted" yet accommodates voice and video comments, which are more commonly found in synchronous or "live" web-conferencing applications (such as Zoom, Adobe Connect, and others). Figure 5.4 provides a view of the VoiceThread interface. When I create a VoiceThread, I view it as a learning activity. I include a title slide, a "Tips for VoiceThread" slide, a slide about grading criteria, and "Instruction" slides that explain precisely what students are expected to do in the VoiceThread. Sometimes I follow these introductory slides with a screencast video I've created (like a mini-lecture), and then I upload slides following the video that contain text-based prompts and images tied back to their reading and the instructional video in the VoiceThread. The students are expected to leave their comments

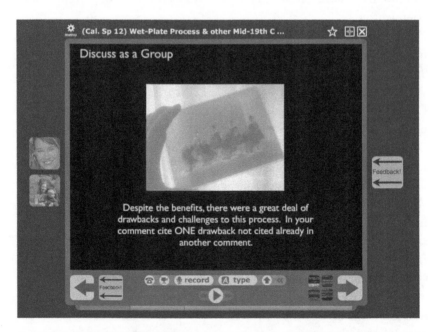

Figure 5.4 Screenshot of a slide from one of my VoiceThread learning activities. Used with permission from VoiceThread, Kim Plowright, author of the glass plate negative photograph, and Kellye Mills.

on the "prompt" slides. The prompts may ask them to summarize a historical photographic process, identify drawbacks or advantages one process had over another, compare and contrast images, analyze historical problems, interpret photographs, or collaboratively summarize contributions made by particular photographers covered in the unit.

I leave it to the students to choose which slides to comment on, and I purposely include more slides than necessary, building in options for students and eliminating redundancy in the contributions. After leaving a comment, the student's profile image appears along the side of the media. Any user can click on the image to play the comment or click the "play" icon at the bottom and sit back as the slide plays like a movie. Listen, read, and watch the comments play—filled with the warmth of your students' presence! As the facilitator, I can easily leave "feedback" comments, which I do using a unique avatar or "identity" within my VoiceThread account. Each VoiceThread account can accommodate many "identities," allowing you to call out your presence clearly on a slide. I also have an identity labeled "Sample Comment" that I use in complex activities so students know exactly what I expect of them.

The "Doodle" tool in VoiceThread is also especially appealing, as it turns each slide into a collaborative whiteboard. For example, in an online art appreciation class, students may be required to view a work of art and, while commenting, use the Doodle tool (activated by using a mouse with the web app or a finger/stylus with the mobile app) to circle an example of an implied line. Simultaneously, in a voice comment, they explain how the implied line they've circled contributes to guiding the viewer's eye through the image (follow this link to see a video demonstrating this activity: youtu.be/yC1NiyOB10A). Essentially, with the Doodle tool, any slide in a VoiceThread becomes a canvas on which you *and* your students can demonstrate mastery of skills.

What's also important to understand is that these learning activities in VoiceThread are peer-to-peer, so the students are doing more than submitting an assignment; they are working together to create content from which the group learns.

VoiceThread has also been an exceptional tool for creating a sense of community in an online class. When surveying my online students, I found that an overwhelming majority agreed that they are more motivated to succeed when they feel like they are part of a community in an online class and that using VoiceThread contributed to establishing a sense of community in the class.[6] A 2011 study by Borup, West, and Graham found that the use of asynchronous video communications improves instructor social presence, which is a student's sense that his/her professor is real and present in a class.[7] Social presence is a key indicator in developing a community of inquiry in online classes.[8]

Moreover, by using VoiceThread's group feature, I have also granted my students "edit" access to a VoiceThread in an effort to allow them to add their own slides with their own media. I call the activity "Visual Thinking," and it is designed to be a student-generated presentation about mid-20th-century photographers, but after the presentation is done, the students re-engage with it and learn from each other's contribution. The mid-20th century is a period that includes a vast array of photographers, and in a traditional teaching environment, I am left to choose which photographers the students will learn about. In an effort to make the instruction more student-centered, I make a list of photographers and share them on a Google Doc (see the "Google Suite" section for more info). The students access the editable document and sign up for the photographer they want to learn more about. Then they proceed to do research about the photographer using Google Books (books.google.com/) and locate two online images by the photographer using Google Image Search (google.com/imghp). After completing the research, their task is to "edit" the VoiceThread and add two slides pertaining to the photographer they chose, with each slide displaying one photograph. The first slide is required to include a 400- to 500-word comment (I require voice or video comments in this activity) that answers the question, "Why is this photographer's work remembered today?" The first slide also has to include a text comment with the citation for the Google Book used in the research. The second slide (containing the second photograph) is designed to be a discussion prompt written by the student.

After the first week of "Visual Thinking," the VoiceThread transforms from a presentation consisting of my introductory and "sample" slides (provided to model my expectations to my students) to a robust presentation of the work of 25 mid-20th century photographers. The second week of the activity requires the students to revisit the VoiceThread, learn about two other photographers, and respond, in voice, to the related discussion prompts. Then the students circle over to their blogs and write a post reflecting on what they learned about the photographers they selected in week two and how the design of the activity allowed them to take control of their learning. It is common for students to note an appreciation for being able to select the photographers who are important to them. Students also expressed that they learned from the challenges they encountered and the need to work through their problems. Some students even noted that they had a newfound appreciation for the amount of work their professors go through to develop their lecture content!

SHOWCASE

Virtual Field Trips with the VoiceThread Mobile App!

Jaime Hannans, a nursing professor at CSU Channel Islands, has designed a VoiceThread activity that gets her students to connect their course curriculum with their local community while constructing knowledge about a topic. The activity was designed with the value of field trips in mind to give students an opportunity to investigate their local community and identify health-related resources. During a module about cardiac health education, Jaime challenged her students to actively explore their local environments and locate an example of 1) an automatic external defibrillator (AED), 2) cardiac health education resources, or 3) public signs or information pertaining to cardiac health education. Students could choose to complete the assignment individually or in a small group. Each student was required to record a video comment. Jaime strongly encouraged students to make their comments on the go, using the VoiceThread mobile app on their phones.

The outcome was quite remarkable. Students recorded video comments from fire stations, gyms, public parking lots, schools, beaches, a farmer's market while describing their journey to locate the resources and capturing their settings on their phones as they spoke. In the end, one of the most surprising wonderful outcomes was the discovery that the location of publicly accessible AEDs varies from county to county. This was discovered because Jaime had students who participated across two distinct counties. To read more details about Jaime's virtual field trip and to see a sample of a student comment, check out the Chapter 5 section of this book's resource site.

Google Suite

Individual educators and entire campuses are adopting Google Suite for teaching and learning. Google Suite is a free collection of communication and collaboration tools. Educational institutions may integrate Google Suite into their campus IT services for free. For those who are not part of an institution that has adopted Google Suite, you may use the tools with your own, individual Google account.

Here is an overview of the major Google Apps (each available in a web and mobile app):

Drive—Drive.Google.com

This is a one-stop online storage solution for your content. Upload photos, documents, videos, and more, and have access to them from anywhere on any device.

Docs—Docs.Google.com

Create an online doc and share it with colleagues or students to generate an instant collaborative writing space. Supports in-line commenting.

Sheets—Docs.Google.com/spreadsheets

These are online collaborative spreadsheets. Follow Alice Keeler (alicekeeler. com) for great Sheets tips!

Slides—Docs.Google.com/presentation

These are online presentations that you may turn into group collaborations. Includes in-line commenting and the option to embed your presentation in any web page.

Forms—Docs.Google.com/forms

These are simple web-based surveys that compile responses into a Google Sheet. This is a terrific resource for collecting student feedback or a quick assessment of student knowledge.

Hangouts—Hangouts.Google.com

Participate in instant one-on-one or group conversations in video, voice, or text.

Sites—Sites.Google.com

The new version of Google Sites allows for you to create beautiful websites with a drag-and-drop interface. Great for student ePortfolios, instructor sites, and more!

 **TIP!**

Use Google Docs for Easy Group Management

Many instructors, like myself, use Google Docs for group management tasks. For example, in my class, I create topics for students to choose from for particular assignments. By listing the topics in a Google Doc spreadsheet and making the page editable to anyone who has access to the link, I can easily include the link in my course shell and allow students to type their names next to the topic of their choice. This empowers them to take control of the project, ensures the list is current, and removes me from the process of updating and managing the progress.

SHOWCASE

Create an Online Icebreaker with Google Slides

I have used Google Slides for an icebreaker in my online History of Photography class. The project, designed in Slides, is titled "My Favorite Photograph," and it invites each student to edit a slide that I have created for them. Upon entering the presentation, the student reads a few preliminary instruction slides explaining how the assignment works, including an opportunity to watch a how-to video that illustrates how to edit the presentation. Then the student locates the slide I have inserted with his/her name on it, adds a favorite photograph, and adds text explaining why he/she selected it. Slowly, throughout the first week of class, the empty presentation slides transform into a beautiful, meaningful collection of images generated by members of the class. The following week, the students return to the presentation and view the completed product. In a blog post, they reflect on what they learned about photographic meaning from this activity. The project is a fun, easy way to engage students in a collaborative activity the first week of class and also engages them in a critical inquiry about the nature of photographic meaning by engaging them with the diverse array of images selected by their peers, which usually include anything from old family photographs, snapshots of children, loved ones away at war, nature landscapes, and works of art. It's a perfect introduction to the class wrapped in an icebreaker that helps students get to know each other.

Finally, if you have a collaborative project in your class (or on campus) in which you are still using a single document that gets edited by multiple people, stop! The most ideal use for Google Docs is to upload an existing document (an MS Word or Excel spreadsheet, for example), adjust the share settings to your preferences, and edit it with your peers. The edits are all collected in a single location, and you can engage in chat with others who are editing the file when you are. In a Google Doc document, use the comment feature to leave sticky note comments that other users can reply to and you can mark as "resolved" once the loose ends are tied up.

Content Curation Tools

The tools shared in this section fall under the umbrella of content curation. A curator is a title granted to individuals employed in a museum whose responsibility it is to identify, select, and acquire objects for inclusion in exhibitions. Curation is a skill that requires an individual to be an expert on a particular topic to effectively assess and validate whether or not an object (or, in our case, an online resource) adds value to the overarching objectives of a collection. As our digital, mobile society continues to inspire and encourage users to create and share content, content curation continues to become an important 21st-century skill. The tools that follow can be used to require students to take on the role of a curator, which involves locating, assessing, and validating resources relevant to a topic and sharing them in some creative ways. All in all, content curation is an area that is growing by leaps and bounds, and many savvy web users are thinking about content curation as the next-generation web search. That is, why enter a few search terms into a web search tool when you can search collections of resources hand-selected by other users?

Bookmarking Apps

Bookmarking applications provide you with a simple method of storing websites that you'd like to revisit later. Some tools, such as Pocket, are simple—placing your saved sites in a feed for you to reference later. Pinterest makes the process visual and makes it easy to share your favorite resources with your networks; while others, such as Diigo and Evernote, allow you to make notes on a web page, snap a photo and tuck it away for later, and share what you've saved with others.

A few favorite content curation apps are

Pocket—GetPocket.com
Diigo—Diigo.com
Evernote—Evernote.com
Pinterest—Pinterest.com

Derek Bruff, referenced earlier in this chapter, has his students at Vanderbilt University use Diigo or Pinterest to identify and examine real-world applications of data visualization and data analysis that reach outside the boundaries of the curriculum covered in his course. Bruff explains to his students that there are three outcomes of the social bookmarking activity:

1. *To help you make connections between the content of this course and other interests of yours, both academic and personal.*
2. *To enrich the learning experience for all of us (including me) in the class.*
3. *Later in the semester, you'll be asked to complete an application project in which you apply the statistical techniques from this course to some "real-world" problem. The collection of examples the class generates through social bookmarking will provide you with lots of potential topics for this project.*[9]

After explaining *how* the tool will enhance the students' learning experience, Bruff gives students an opportunity to evaluate both Diigo and Pinterest, and to select the tool they prefer. Then he introduces students to the bookmarking process and begins to give assignments to the class requiring them to use the tool of their choice with clear instructions about how to tag the bookmarks in both tools. The first bookmarking assignment he gives is

- *Find and bookmark an example of data visualization. The more complex the data, the better.*
- *For Diigo users, tag your bookmark with "dataviz." For Pinterest users, include the hashtag "#dataviz" in your bookmark's description.*

By scaffolding the students' exposure to and use of a new tool, openly sharing outcomes, and including himself in the learning community, Bruff demonstrates an effective integration of an emerging technology that is driven by pedagogy. The collections generated by the students are shared with the class, thus empowering students to become the creators of the course content from which they learn.

Scoop.it

 Scoop.it

Feature Overview

- Select a topic and collect links about that topic arranged in a visual online magazine format.
- Free tool with premium options.
- Make curation collaborative by granting permission to other users to add posts to your topic.
- Leave comments on any item in a topic.
- Auto-share to social media tools (for example, your Facebook or Twitter account).
- Mobile app available for iPhone and iPad.

Scoop.it is a site that can be used to create a magazine-like collection of web resources that support any given topic. You can also use Scoop.it to follow topics curated by other users. After selecting your topic, you will be able to review suggested resources via the dashboard page in Scoop.it. The suggested resources are mined from sources that you can customize (for example, you can add a Twitter user who is an expert on the topic or delete any of the sources Scoop.it has recommended). As topics are suggested, you select which ones you want to add as posts within your topic.

With a free account, a user can curate up to five collections, and this number increases if you upgrade to one of the premium account options. And, as the lead creator of a Scoop.it topic, you can add emails of additional users who you'd like to be able to add posts to your collection.

 TIP!

Use Bookmarklets for Fast and Easy Curation!

As you begin to get your arms around using Scoop.it or any other content curation tool, the quality of your experience as well as your content will improve by using the tool's bookmarklet. A bookmarklet is a little application that you can simply drag and drop into the top of your browser (in the bookmark bar). Once it's installed there, you can click on it to seamlessly add a web page you are on to the collection you're curating with that specific tool.

Assessing Participatory Learning

Identifying a plan for grading the work that students contribute in response to participatory learning activities can be baffling at first. The key is to step back and don't let the digital format of their work throw you for a loop. Just because there isn't a tangible stack of papers in front of you to grade doesn't mean there isn't evidence of learning. Instead, as you develop an activity (or a series of activities for a course), keep an eye on what the learning outcomes are. More specifically, identify exactly what the students are 1) required to do and 2) how their contributions will demonstrate what they've learned. Then organize this information into a rubric and share the rubric with students prior to the initiation of the activity or project.

To help you get started with creating rubrics for participatory, digital learning activities, you may find it helpful to view some samples. The Eberly Center for Teaching and Learning at Carnegie Mellon shares many fine examples of rubrics for a variety of projects and activities for different disciplines (cmu.edu/teaching/assessment/examples/courselevel-bycollege/index.html). According to the Eberly Center, a rubric should contain:

- Criteria: the aspects of performance (e.g., argument, evidence, clarity) that will be assessed
- Descriptors: the characteristics associated with each dimension (e.g., argument is demonstrable and original, evidence is diverse and compelling)
- Performance levels: a rating scale that identifies students' level of mastery within each criterion

The sample rubric shared in Figure 5.5 is one that I have used to assess VoiceThread activities in my online class that I use as general formative assessments. In these activities, students listen to my instructions, view a mini video lecture/presentation, and respond to prompts I have written. They receive up to 10 points for their contributions, and they are graded on three criteria: originality, comprehension, and clarity.

The Role of Social Media in the Future of College Learning

How will emerging technologies reshape the future of college learning? That's an exciting question to ponder, and in the case studies included in this chapter, we can see some glimpses into the future. It is likely that we will continue to see more professors who steer away from textbooks for providing course

	Exemplary - 3.33	Developing - 2	Beginning - 1	No Credit - 0	Score
Originality	The minimum number of comments are left and all comments are in the student's own words and contribute unique viewpoints or ideas.	Comment(s) are in the student's own words and contribute mostly unique viewpoints or ideas.	Student comment(s) demonstrate repetition of ideas contributed in previous comments.	Student comment(s) demonstrate evidence of plagiarism.	
Comprehension	The minimum number of comments are left and all comments demonstrate an understanding of the related concepts and ideas and may demonstrate an effort to build on previous students comments left on the slide.	Comment(s) demonstrate an attempt to understand the related concepts and ideas.	Comment(s) demonstrate little to no understanding of the related concepts and ideas.	Student comment(s) demonstrate evidence of plagiarism.	
Clarity	The minimum number of comments are left and all comments are clear and understandable.	Written or spoken comments are mostly clear and understandable.	Written or spoken comments are not clear or understandable.	Student comment(s) demonstrate evidence of plagiarism.	

Figure 5.5 Rubric sample.

content and experiment more with connecting students to user-generated content in an effort to engage them in a critical inquiry about particular topics or problems.

Jason Rosenblum, associate director for the Center for Teaching and Learning at the New York Institute for Technology, has taken an intriguing approach to using social media in teaching. Rosenblum worked with Robert Strong, a professor in University Programs at St. Edward's University, to design and facilitate a course about global social problems. As they designed the course, the two embraced a gameful approach by challenging students to complete a series of three missions—to research global social problems, take action (online and face-to-face) to deal with those problems, and, finally, imagine potential solutions for those problems to successfully complete the course. As Rosenblum points out,

> Our course was heavily inspired by the work of Jane McGonigal (Jane Mcgonigal.com/) and her work to inspire gameful participation to deal with real-life social issues in her alternate realty game (ARG), Evoke (Urgent.Evoke.com). We wanted to challenge people to take Heroic action to deal with serious global social problems. We incorporated social media in significant ways in the course; first, as a tool for research and second as a tool to take action to deal with their chosen problem. Students used social media tools such as Twitter, Facebook, Mashable, Evri and Scoop.it to research and take action to deal with problems that included water security, gender inequality, poverty, and the war in the Democratic Republic of the Congo. Students even participated in the live stream of the Social Good Summit, an event that highlighted the importance of using technology such as social media, for social good (Mashable.com/sgs/). All course participation was public on the course site, and students were required to write blog posts and reflections based on their research and social media activities. Our goal was to design a class in which course participation was grounded in a set of Heroic Character Traits (e.g. tenacity, courage, empathy, credibility, etc.), and in which the assessment for every course activity was relevant and authentic.

In Rosenblum and Strong's model, students learn how to locate pertinent information, examine the conversations, and think critically about them. Examples of this can be found through social media activities in the action mission, where students were asked to locate articles online that were pertinent to their chosen global social issues. Students then needed to post a comment to those articles and to write a blog entry that demonstrated a reflection of their process to critically evaluate and respond to those articles online. In one instance, a student chose to respond to an article about birth control on the *New York Times'* website comment area. This student's comment was not only subsequently "recommended" by over 40 other readers but also the *Times* decided to promote the comment by making it one of a smaller number of "Highlighted" comments on a popular *Times* article.

Successful completion of the missions in the course was evaluated through a series of rubrics that emphasized students' ability to critically analyze and synthesize material from research and activities that involved not only traditional academic sources but also social media sources including Facebook, Twitter, and a variety of other online socially enabled content. All course outcomes were designed to be authentic. According to Rosenblum,

> As educators we should inquire—early and often—what it means for students to live and learn in a globally-connected world. How can we help students to develop the critical literacies they need to not only consume content, but also create knowledge?

These learning outcomes are, arguably, essential 21st-century literacies for students living in a mobile, digital world. As they embark on their missions, students become active participants in existing online conversations about a topic of their choice, and they are also empowered to begin and lead new conversations. Their quest is to change the world—quite a lofty objective for a college course, I'd say.

Rosenblum and Strong created a web page to communicate the course policy about how their students are expected to use social media in the class. Students are required to connect their Twitter accounts to the course website and to tweet their blog postings using the course hashtag, #globsoc. In addition, students are strongly encouraged to use Twitter for research and to share information relevant to their topics through tweets and retweets, finding and following Twitter users who share content related to their topic, creating lists to organize content, and sharing other course-related content with the #globsoc hashtag. Students are also encouraged to use Facebook to research the activities of non-profit organizations and other users that are relevant to their selected topic. The course policy web page includes best practices and information about university policies. Expectations are clearly communicated upfront—an essential part of teaching effectively with emerging technologies. And what of the student experience? The course instructors provided one quote by a student who described the overall course experience.

> I got a lot out of this course. I have always been a very passionate person with anything that I've ever set my mind to, whether it be my career in the arts or my school work. This class was a wonderful way to make people really work to change the world, and not just to write one more paper on it. I was able to reach out and actually change lives in this course and that is amazing.

All in all, this approach to learning empowers students to become actively involved with real-world scenarios and learn that they really can make a difference. Through their participation through Twitter, Facebook, and other social media tools, they learn, through experience, the power that social media holds for giving each member of our society a voice. They learn how their participation in social media can contribute to changing the world, as opposed to using it to inform the world about what they had for dinner.

Summary

Building off the momentum we established in Chapter 4, this chapter has augmented your teaching toolkit to include an array of social technologies, many of which are supported with mobile apps, that offer options for creating student-centered learning activities. The tools here are merely colors in a palette. Like an artist, your task is to select a tool and align it with your own creative vision to construct relevant, engaging learning activities for your students.

In Chapter 6, we will build upon our momentum further by maintaining a focus on collaborative, participatory learning but shifting the emphasis to teaching and learning in the public web. Chapter 6 examines how our mobile, social era is affecting the nature of the LMS and encouraging more faculty to consider stepping outside its secure walls to teach in the open web.

Notes

1. *Twitter Website*. Retrieved on July 25, 2016 from https://about.twitter.com/company.
2. Duggan, M., Ellison, N. B., Lampe, C., Lenhart, A., & Madden, M. (2015). Social Media Update 2014. *Pew Research Center*. Retrieved from www.pewinternet.org/2015/01/09/demographics-of-key-social-networking-platforms-2/.
3. Atkinson, C. (2009). *How People Are using Twitter and Social Media and Changing Presentations Forever*. Berkeley, CA: New Riders Press.

4. Bruff, D. (2011, May 17). Backchannel (and me) in the New York Times. *Agile Learning* [blog post]. Retrieved from http://derekbruff.org/?p=979.
5. Davidson, C. & Goldbert, D. T. (2010). *The Future of Thinking: Learning Institutions in a Digital Age.* Cambridge, MA: The MIT Press.
6. To view a VoiceThread I created to showcase examples of how I've used Voice-Thread in my classes, excerpts of student contributions, student feedback about VoiceThread, and survey results about VoiceThread, go to http://voicethread.com/share/908650/.
7. Borup, J., West, R. E., & Graham, C. R. (2011). Improving Online Social Presence through Asynchronous Video. *Internet and Higher Education*, 15 (3): 195–203.
8. Garrison, D. R., Anderson, T., & Archer, W. (2000). Critical Inquiry in a Text-based Environment: Computer Conferencing in Higher Education. *The Internet and Higher Education*, 2 (2–3): 87–105.
9. Bruff, D. (2012, January 8). *Social Bookmarking 101. Math 216: Statistics for Engineering* [blog post]. Retrieved from http://derekbruff.org/blogs/math216/?p=52.

Chapter 6

Unlocking Learning

The illiterate of the 21st century will not be those who cannot read and write, but those who cannot learn, unlearn, and relearn.

—Alvin Toffler

The pages of this book have demonstrated the potential emerging technologies hold for making student learning more active, relevant, and engaging. The technologies that have been featured in this book enable opportunities for developing online content that is visually appealing and rich with human presence, as well as connecting individuals across distances in conversations, reflections, and professional learning networks. If you are a faculty member who has always taught with the traditional toolkit used in higher education—a textbook from an academic publisher and a LMS—you may view these tools as pathways to unlock your students' learning and to connect with them in new ways.

This has certainly been my own pathway into teaching with emerging technologies. When I started teaching online in an LMS, I was disappointed in the quality of the learning environment I had developed for my students and felt constrained by features available to me. By experimenting with new tools, I discovered different ways of engaging my students and opportunities for being present in their learning. But I still felt the *need* to use an LMS, largely because of concerns about violating the license for the images included in the textbook I was using, as well as my (former) institution's expectation for faculty to teach with institutionally supported technologies. I imagine many instructors can relate to that experience.

The LMS has become incredibly pervasive in higher education, and its extensive use may be contributing to a gap between the skills college graduates *need* and the skills they *have*. When students graduate from college, they are expected to demonstrate to prospective employers how their skills set themselves apart from others. Doing this requires individuals to have a digital identity, which involves, first, being familiar with one's personal strengths and passions and creating digital media to communicate them to a public audience. Creating one's digital identity also requires knowledge of how the web works. Yet few four-year degree patterns bundle these skills within a degree program.

At the time of writing, the increased adoption of web-based technologies in higher education is making an impact on the LMS marketplace. Early adopter faculty who teach with an LMS and use web-based tools have struggled with finding a way to integrate these technologies seamlessly into their students' learning experiences. As Phil Hill, consultant and industry analyst, explains,

> The LMS does a very poor job at providing a lot of learning technologies desired by faculty and students. There is no way that a monolithic LMS can keep up with the market—it cannot match functionality of open internet tools.[1]

Hill goes on to explain how LMS vendors attempted to replicate the functionality of web-based technologies most desired by faculty and students by creating imitations of these tools and including them inside the LMS. This approach was necessary to sustain the traditional model of the LMS, which has functioned very much like a "walled garden."[2]

However, this approach didn't work well, resulting in what Hill calls "feature bloat." Alternatively, LMSs are now embracing interoperability as a key feature, which simply means providing more effective ways to integrate external tools. Learning Tools Interoperability (LTI), is an industry standard developed by IMS Global Learning Consortium, which enables a secure exchange of information between an external tool provider and the LMS. With LTI, an LMS plays nicely with outside tools: assignments that use external tools can be configured from within the LMS, assignments can be assessed from the LMS gradebook, and single sign-on can be integrated too, thus eliminating the requirement for faculty and students to have multiple accounts. These plug-and-play features are referred to as interoperability in educational technology lingo. In short, LTI is paving a way for the LMS to co-exist with web-based technologies. Inserting windows and doors into the walls of the LMS is now an option.

The LMS marketplace is changing, but, nonetheless, the pervasive use of LMSs in higher education has generated a monolithic mind-set about how to teach online and blended classes. There are alternatives. In this chapter, we will investigate some of the alternative practices that support the development of digital literacy and digital identity in students *and faculty*. Faculty members who have always taught in an LMS have not been immersed in the inner workings of the web, and this is a problem. Faculty must possess particular skills before they can begin to model them and foster them in their students. But the reality is that teaching in the public web is a fragile topic. When a faculty member makes the leap to subvert tradition and teach outside an LMS, she is likely to receive a cold response from colleagues. While writing this book, for example, I connected with a university professor who was told by a peer to stop having her students use Twitter in her online classes, as it was just "too much" for them. This individual, who preferred to remain anonymous, is a part-time instructor vying for a full-time position. As a result, she elected to scale back her use of social media in her classes, despite believing that using social technologies can improve students' digital literacy and help them to construct a digital identity.

This chapter will provide an introduction to some alternatives to the traditional toolkit. It is my hope that this chapter will encourage a new way of thinking about the technologies employed in teaching and learning and, possibly, start conversations on campus about whether or not the students who graduate from your campus this year will be prepared for a meaningful, productive future.

In the pages that follow, we will delve into the fringes of higher education, where there are communities of professors, instructional designers, educational technologists, administrators, and students exploring the implications of what it means for college students to learn in their own public web space (or domain) and leverage open educational resources (OERs) in place of commercial textbooks.

Rethinking the LMS

The higher education LMS market began to develop after access to the web became widely available. An LMS, also referred to as a course management system (CMS) and a virtual learning environment in the United Kingdom, was conceived to be a centralized web-based location for instructors to organize content and share it with their students beyond the walls of a classroom. In many ways, an LMS is a digital version of a classroom—a place to present information and resources, communicate to students and to enable student-student interactions (discussion forums, blogs, and wikis). Much like the walls of a classroom, an LMS segregates content and conversations inside a secure space, dislocating learning from the public web. If one of the purposes of college is preparing students for success in the real world—which is profoundly different from the world that most faculty entered after graduation—we must ponder if requiring faculty to teach in an LMS is what's truly best for our students. What alternatives are there?

Once upon a time, college instructors who were interested in enhancing their students' learning with web-based technologies did not have access to an LMS such as Blackboard, Web CT, Moodle, Sakai, or Desire2Learn. For many of us, it may seem difficult to wrap our minds around what this experience must have been like. After all, in 2003, just six years after the higher education LMS market was established, more than 90% of higher education institutions had adopted an LMS.[3] Jim Groom, an educator, educational technologist, and entrepreneur who will be referenced multiple times in this chapter, views the LMS as higher education's "solution to the web," which, in turn, undermines the potential for innovations in teaching and learning.[4] The web is a messy, interconnected hub that disseminates knowledge contributed by individuals from around the world. In many ways, it seems like the democratic nature of the web should be received as a dream come true for an educator. However, the untamed nature of web-based interactions stands in sharp contrast to the structured type of learning that occurs in an LMS.

In contrast, many educators value the LMS for bringing consistency to the student learning experience. Some feel that the LMS is an essential tool for enabling copyrighted content to be re-used for academic purposes and made viewable only to registered students. Another argument for the LMS is that it protects student information that may otherwise violate federal student privacy laws (FERPA). In short, the LMS is a technology deeply informed by the call for accountability in higher education.

Other educators, however, are critical of efforts to manage learning. After all, learning is, by nature, a complex process. It is social, involves emotions, and evolves over time in a rhythm that is unique to each person. Jennifer Ross and Amy Collier see emerging technologies as an opportunity to explore the messiness of learning, and they are critical of technologies that aim to simplify its natural unruliness. Ross and Collier note, "Working with mess in an age of accountability means acknowledging that learners, too, have complex identities and are embodied in various ways."[5] Collier and Ross explicitly take note of the tendency for educational technology companies to tout how their products help instructors save time, be more efficient, capture data to unveil trends, etc. Similarly, when an instructor is provided an empty course shell to design a course and teach students, that environment is regulated by a set of rules—things that an instructor can and cannot do—which sets rules for students as well.

In an LMS, the rigidity of the technology determines *who* your students can interact with, *how* they may express themselves, and *what* content they may engage with. For example, when I use Blackboard, I can choose to use folders or the learning modules feature to arrange the content with which I want my students to engage. I could choose to set up a link for my students that would take them outside an LMS into the public web. But when we are used to teaching in an LMS, we understand these moments as intrusions that need to be tamed (for example, embedding content in an LMS instead of linking out to content).

What if these unwelcome intrusions are, instead, pathways to learning that offer students opportunities to foster skills necessary for succeeding in a digital society? What other types of content and dialogue might a student encounter upon clicking a link that takes her into the web? How might this affect her perception and understanding of the course topics? What choices might she need to make about where she clicks, who she interacts with, and what she chooses to share? Are these scenarios to be avoided, or are they opportunities for students to learn how to foster relevant life skills?

Embracing the Potential of Messiness

Laura Gibbs, an online instructor at the University of Oklahoma, embraces the messiness of the public web to create relevant learning experiences that foster her students' creativity and critical-thinking skills. Gibbs teaches two online classes, Mythology and Folklore and Indian Epics. Her institution has used the LMS, Desire2Learn (D2L), for more than 10 years and, at the time of writing, is in the process of transitioning their campus LMS to Canvas. However, unlike most faculty at her institution, Gibbs does not teach her classes in an LMS. She explains,

> I have no use for an LMS, aside from using it to communicate grades to my students. If I have my students do something, I want it to be really useful to them and to others, but if you put a class in an LMS, it's not useful to anyone.

To Gibbs, an LMS is like a "locked filing cabinet": it is good at providing a place for instructors to store confidential information, such as grades, for students. Aside from that, she has no use for an LMS in the design of her classes. Gibbs started teaching traditional, face-to-face classes in 1999. She reflects, "Back then we didn't have Blackboard or any LMS at all at my institution. Instead, we had a funky, homegrown photo roster of students and a links board.

That was all faculty had." At that time, Laura was already tinkering with the possibilities of enhancing her students' learning with the web. She reflects, "Even before I taught online, the web was an essential part of every class." Her institution provided faculty and students with 3MB of web space, which wouldn't be enough to do anything meaningful with these days, but back then it was enough to host a site! In 2002, when she started teaching online, she kept building upon the blended learning strategies she had in place.

In the design of her course, she uses a combination of blogs, wikis, Google Docs, Twitter, Diigo, Pinterest, and YouTube to share content with her students and pulls it all together in a single website at MythFolklore.net/. From there, students may click out to supporting sites for their particular class, which include a class announcements site, online syllabi, OERs (see later in this chapter), blogs from current students, samples of former student work, reflections from past students, and more.

So in what way does Gibbs use an LMS then? At the time of writing, Gibbs is using Canvas, her institution's newly adopted LMS, to provide a simple, clear framework for her students. Unlike other LMSs, Canvas gives instructors the option to make the content within a course fully public (if the course includes student contributions and grades, these items remain secure and visible only to those enrolled in the course after they authenticate into Canvas). If you'd like to see the framework of her courses in Canvas, go to Myth.MythFolklore.net and India.MythFolklore.net. These links take you (and her students) directly to the course announcements page.

I visited Laura's course page as the semester was unfolding. When I clicked on the link, Canvas opened without a prompt to log in. I was greeted with a friendly written welcome announcement and much more! On the course homepage (where her blog is embedded), there is some content that changes. This dynamic content consists of content feeds that stream in from various external sites. One feed shows tweets sent by Laura via the course Twitter account, as well as tweets by students that Laura has retweeted (see Figure 6.1). There is also a motivational image (or meme) that changes each time the page loads. Laura used the tool RotateContent.com to add the rotating images feature (by the way, this tool was created by one of Laura's former students). The image that appears relays an inspirational message that relates to Carol Dweck's growth mind-set. At the time of writing, I was presented with an image of two Siamese kittens playing with toilet paper rolls that read, "We do things better . . . together." Students who click on the "more info" link near the cat image are taken to the growth mind-set blog, which includes a collection of fun and inspirational messages, as well as challenges that encourage students to

Heather Sizemore @HeatherSize76 · Aug 23
I am loving my Mythology and Folklore course with Professor Laura Gibbs
@OnlineMythIndia #OU3043

Figure 6.1 Tweet sent from one of Laura Gibbs's students containing the course hashtag. Printed with permission from Heather Sizemore.

conceive of learning as a lifelong journey that they are in control of, as opposed to something some people are good or bad at.

At the end of Gibbs's first course announcement, students are offered the chance to view a video embedded from YouTube of Mr. Rogers reminding us all, "You can grow ideas in the garden of your mind. It's good to be curious about many things." That video represents Gibbs's teaching philosophy, views of education, and technologies she chooses to use in her teaching. In Gibbs's class, open-ended assignments put students in the position of making choices, which promotes problem-solving and creativity skills.

Each week, Gibbs's students read fables, fairy tales, and other traditional stories by clicking on links to websites. Students create their own blogs on which they make several posts each week: they share their reading notes, a story that they have written based on the reading, and other research and reflection posts. In the weekly storytelling post, students step into the role of storyteller by choosing one story from the course materials, and in their own writing, tell the story through a unique lens. For example, a student may tell a story through the perspective of a minor character, requiring students to engage deeply with the narrative, analyze the characteristics of other characters, and create a unique twist on an old fable.

You may be asking, however, "Why can't this be done in an LMS?" Well, some of it could be done in an LMS, but it would change the student experience immensely. Gibbs explains,

> I want the students to be able to share not just with each other, but also with their friends and families. They frequently report doing this and I can tell they are happy and proud about doing so. Also, students enrolled in my two separate classes interact with each other, which would not be possible if the course was taught in a traditional LMS, as the classes would be walled off from one another. Students are also very aware that future students will read their work since I rely heavily on past student work as part of the course content.

In short, the activities that Gibbs's students participate in are not *disposable* like nearly all their other course work is and has been prior to college. Robin DeRosa, professor and director of interdisciplinary studies at Plymouth State University, who also teaches in the public web, shared via Twitter, "My class could remember only one 'non-disposable' assignment from high school: a teacher kept one student's project as a 'bad example' for future students." A non-disposable assignment, in our context, is work a student produces that has a life beyond the end of the class. Every year when the school year ends, my own children come home, empty the contents of their backpacks onto the floor, and there it sits—until I throw it away. When faculty design classes in a secure LMS, they are dislocating themselves from the immense possibilities that the web holds for designing meaningful activities that result in work students can share and be proud of.

Beyond increasing motivation through non-disposable assignments, participating in the public web immerses individuals in the process of navigating today's digital landscape. Creating and sharing content and responding to comments online is how one learns to become digitally literate and masters digital citizenship skills. When I was young, I remember sitting in a classroom listening to a presentation about how to be safe in public places. I was informed about the risks of speaking to strangers and taught how to identify safe places in my community where I could turn for help. However, none of that information would have been useful to me if I hadn't had the opportunity to walk through my neighborhood, go to the park, or hang out at the mall with my friends.

Similarly, some of the most powerful learning experiences I had in college involved leaving my classroom and applying what I was learning to my surroundings. For example, as an undergraduate in a beginning drawing class, I remember listening to a lecture about linear perspective, which is a formula that artists have used since the 15th century to represent the illusion of three-dimensional space on a two-dimensional surface (paper, canvas, etc.). I remember sitting inside the student union with my drawing board on my lap, analyzing the lines along the top and bottom of the hallway that extended in front of me. I remember identifying where the "vanishing point" and "orthogonals" were in my own surroundings and replicating them on my paper. As I developed my drawing, I began to understand the concept of linear perspective at a deep level, and I also viewed paintings in my art history class entirely differently. The point here is that taking students outside the walls of a classroom has always been a powerful teaching practice.

As Gibbs's class unfolds, students spend the first week completing an orientation of sorts that functions like a living syllabus. That is, instead of reading what the course will consist of, they do it. And by the end of the week, students are in full swing. To get started, students view a clear, organized outline that details what they need to do each day of the week. But this structured outline is packed with choices, requiring students to make decisions about their own learning from the outset. For example, on Tuesday, students are assigned to "design your course," "create your blog," and make a first post on the blog that describes "a favorite place." The heart of her class for students is the Storybook project, which involves creating a website that showcases a collection of stories, written by the student-author, that are aligned with a particular theme. Students may also opt to create a portfolio project instead, which is a series of their best stories written during the class, improved through many revisions. To view a large collection of storybooks from Laura's past students, go to this link: StoryBooks.MythFolklore.net.

As I engaged with Gibbs's course workflow and projects, I began to understand that her course design intentionally immerses her students in an organized mess to guide them into the driver's seat of their own learning. She has developed a framework for students that presents them with a buffet of topics, themes, and projects from which they piece together their learning plan for the class. As students embark on their own learning design, they learn about myths, fables, and epics; hone their writing skills; and develop digital literacy.

As I ponder Laura Gibbs's class, I am impressed with the time and commitment she dedicates to her online classes. She is incredibly present in her students' learning (which is a hallmark of any great online learning experience), and all of us can see this presence, given her option to teach in the public web. I am also pulled into a reflection about the digital citizenship skills fostered through Laura's course. Students are learning how to appropriately participate in online conversations, re-use content appropriately, design, and create a website, as well as create a blog. Beyond all of the "how-tos," however, they learn how it feels to make contributions to the web. As Gibbs explains, "My goal is for my students to re-vision the impersonal vastness of the Internet into something they create and benefit from: their own learning network." These are not skills and experiences that most college students master in higher education. If college and university faculty were not given a shell in an LMS to teach each online class, perhaps they would likely, instead, be learning how to build and share content in the public, like Laura Gibbs, and modeling these skills to their students.

Developing Digital Identity, Digital Literacy, and Creativity through a Domain of One's Own

Laura Gibbs's approach to course design is unique; however, she did not develop her approach independently. Several years after she started teaching online, Gibbs heard about an open online course about digital storytelling, called DS106, offered through the University of Mary Washington. It wasn't just a typical course; however, it was a course that was taught in the public web and anyone could participate or follow along. Laura did not enroll; she lurked. Along with many others from around the world, she followed the class dialogue across blogs and Twitter and interacted with the course facilitators. By having the opportunity to slip right into this public course, Gibbs learned a great deal about how to design a student-centered learning experience that embraces the hyperlinked nature of the web.

The story about how DS106 got started loops back to 2007 when the University of Mary Washington embarked upon the creation of an institutional blogging system that became known as UMW Blogs. Essentially, the project involved the creation of a WordPress Multisite, which allowed all at the institution to generate their own WordPress blog, which came along with a collection of themes and plug-ins provided by the institution. WordPress is an open source blogging platform that is used heavily in industry, as well as education, to provide a fairly straightforward method of creating a website. Plug-ins for WordPress are developed by the user community and offer an endless array of options for customizing the look, feel, and functionality of a site. UMW students used WordPress to create websites that served as literary journals, online exhibits, poetry publications, and interconnected spaces to converse with authors of the works they were reading.[6]

In 2011, UMW Blogs was an inspiration for a computer science class about digital storytelling, DS106 (#DS106), taught by Jim Groom and several other faculty at the same institution. DS106 is not a typical online class. In fact, it is, by nature, designed to encourage participants to question all things "typical." Consequently, unlike most classes about digital storytelling, this class does not define what storytelling is; instead, it is more of a postmodern deconstruction of the topic.

Students of DS106 engage in a self-directed journey that examines how the web works and how meaning is produced. Anyone may participate in DS106 with UMW students, and participants are encouraged to engage with the parts of the course that interest them. The open nature of the course has attracted other institutions around the world teaching similar courses. The participant experience consists of layers—each person chooses his/her pathway, which is both fueled by the web and a part of the web. To participate, one is expected to acquire (or already have) their own web space or domain. In their web space, participants create content independently on sites that are their own. Groom and his fellow course assistants used syndication as a method to curate the student content onto a main course portal (DS106.us/flow/). Syndication allows for portions of a website's content to be made available to other websites through the use of feeds. To be clear, syndication merely provides a way of collecting and presenting content, but the actual look/feel and functionality of the students' sites is driven entirely by student choice.

Standardization is avoided in DS106. In fact, students are encouraged to submit ideas for assignments to the DS106 Assignment Bank (Assignments.DS106.us/). Assignments are contributed and tagged by assignment type (visual, design, audio, video, web, mashup, etc.). Participants are invited to share feedback, ideas, and tutorials to each assignment page to improve the experience of future students. At the time of writing, the Assignment Bank contained about 1,000 assignments, and 11,000 assignments have been submitted.[7]

After an assignment is added to the bank, class participants may rate its difficulty by assigning one to five stars. Then, for a particular course topic, participants are instructed to complete, for example, 10 stars of web assignments. This approach allows students to choose the assignments that are the most intriguing and relevant to them. For example, by clicking on "Web Assignments" from the Assignment Bank, students may choose from an array of options: to earn four stars, create a mind map that visually communicates how things and entities are interconnected (contributed by Stephen Rechter); three stars for contributing a comment onto the page of a product on Amazon or eBay to understand how comments can function as mini-stories (contributed by Adam Levine); or for four stars, write a post that examines the motives that inspired a group to come together (contributed by Lesya Melnychenko). Upon completing an assignment, participants create a new post on their blogs about the assignment and add tags to the post (provided on the assignment page), which ensure the posts are auto-populated into the course syndication feed. Participants also join in on the Daily Create projects, each of which are designed to take 20 minutes or less. Each day, a new create prompt is posted (Daily.DS106.us), students respond (usually by writing a blog post, creating an image, recording a video), and share their creation from Twitter with the designated hashtag (search for #tdc1692 on Twitter to view recent contributions).

DS106 demonstrates the potential of the web's messiness to provide endless opportunities for creative, collaborative, and self-directed learning. As Emily Strong, a former DS106 student shares,

> Between daily creates and projects from the assignment bank, I am constantly creating things, and I find myself taking more creative approaches to everything else in my life, from approaching problems at work to noticing the interesting angles and textures of a room.[8]

Yet DS106 has also contributed to the professional development of other faculty as well. It has served as an inspiration for countless educators to understand a way to teach *with* the web, as opposed to *against* the web in an LMS. As Laura Gibbs notes, "Because DS106 was a public course, I was able to watch and learn from it along every step of my own online teaching journey." Unlocking learning is a key to promoting innovations in teaching and learning, as well as developing meaningful, relevant skills for students.

You may be wondering how having students post their work in the public web, in general, is permissible under FERPA (Family Educational Rights and Privacy Act) guidelines. FERPA was founded on ensuring students are in control of their own data or "student records" (and exactly what constitutes a record may vary and is often debated). FERPA requires students to "opt in" to any public sharing of information. When designing learning activities that involve participating in the public web, it's essential to clearly communicate the public nature of the activities to students and provide those who prefer *not* to participate an alternative option. WordPress, the software most commonly used for blogging in DoOO, may be set up to be public or password protected, proving a simple alternative. Another option is to allow students to publish their web-based work anonymously, with a pseudonym, or with their initials. Laura Gibbs shares, "Quite a few of my students do not put their name on their Storybook website and that's fine. It's their choice."

The early success of DS106 inspired yet another experiment at UMW. In 2012, Groom and his colleagues, Martha Burtis, Tim Owens, and others, began a project titled Domain of One's Own (DoOO), which would provide incoming UMW students with a method of obtaining their own domain for the duration of their time at UMW. As Morgen and Rorabough explain, DoOO is a method for "educating students and faculty about the essential building blocks of the web and encouraging them to take an active role in the construction of their own digital identity."[9]

Haley Campbell was a student in DS106 in the fall of 2012 and created her own domain in the class. She had just started her senior year at UMW and was feeling the pressure of her looming graduation. As she prepared her class schedule, she recalls hearing about a "very challenging, wildly fun" class that "involved making your own GIFs." "What could be better?" she thought. So she enrolled in DS106. Prior to DS106, most, if not all, of Haley's college classes involved the use of Canvas, a major LMS, to some degree. While she was in high school, Blackboard was the standard. Haley says the difference between DS106 and her other classes was like "night and day." Most of her instructors utilized Canvas as a repository for documents, as opposed to a learning environment, she shares. However, she has seen classes that used an LMS for student-student interactions, and she describes them as "flat" and the discussions as "hard to follow." She continues by stating that in those classes "there was . . . no sense of who the students were as people or what had informed their responses to the readings." There was also very little instructor presence.

In contrast, in DS106 Haley's professors were available through multiple social media networks as well as through traditional email. They chimed in regularly on student blog posts to provide ongoing support through the development of ideas and project. Haley reflects on how the use of Twitter, blog comments, and Google Hangouts provided a "less formal" way for her to communicate with her professors. She explains,

> Communicating with a professor through an LMS *feels* more serious by virtue of the format itself, while the ease of sending a quick tweet to a professor and looping in the rest of the #ds106 community for feedback resulted in better dialogue.

Beyond communication, however, Haley noticed a distinct difference in the process of completing assignments. Instead of opening a module, viewing a prescribed list of what to do, doing it on her own, and submitting it to her professor by a due date, completing assignments in DS106 was an experience to "be shared, explained, discussed, and ultimately lauded publicly," especially if the end product was "something awesome." Haley embarked upon her assignments with creative freedom, as she was granted the ability to choose what to do from the Assignment Bank. She explains, "While the format [of DS106] is certainly more challenging for a lot of students, it made my assignments feel more valuable than hitting 'Upload File' and waiting for a grade."

The reflections that Haley shared about her experiences in DS106 align directly with effective online teaching practices. A strong instructor presence, regular feedback, and student-student interactions are foundations of high-quality online teaching and learning and mastering these elements can be achieved in an LMS or in the public web. So what impact did owning her domain have on her learning? She shares,

> Prior to DS106, I'd never had a .com to call my own, and hadn't thought I needed one. If all I needed was a blog to ramble on and there was a service available that would let me build one for free, why go beyond that? 'Ownership' wasn't on my radar, probably because I never examined the fact that I didn't really 'own' the digital platforms I was using.

This observation made by Haley is one that likely would not have been realized if DS106 was taught in an LMS or even with UMW Blogs. By creating her own web space, Haley was able to see that other spaces in which she participates are controlled, governed, and owned by profit-making companies. Like most students who don't remember life before the Internet, Haley had never considered the complexities involved with participating in the web. By creating accounts and contributing content, users are directly playing a role in the profit-making efforts of companies, even if the tools we use are free. By participating on Facebook, for example, I provide information about my interests and preferences to Facebook and the web of companies that pay for a presence in my feed. By participating in "my" Facebook account, I contribute data that is used by companies to improve their products. DoOO fosters a critical awareness of the political and economic power embedded in the web's infrastructure. As Morgen and Rorabough explain,

> DoOO takes the approach that large corporations are not the only ones that can assert agency on the web . . . and that students who develop digital literacies begin to see the web differently, as less of a consumer space and more useful for meaningful learning and interaction.[10]

DoOO is alive and strong at UMW. Students have used it to share their research, create ePortfolios of artwork, showcase historic preservation work, blog about their world travels, and develop an online literary journal (to view examples, go to UMW.Domains). And DoOO is spreading! At the time of writing, 33 institutions of higher education offer a DoOO option to their students and faculty. As the project expands, more faculty and students are receiving their own space to write, their own space to create, and their own space to develop a digital presence. The impact is not known, as this is an experiment. We are seeing students step into a critical conversation about DoOO too. For example, Andrew Rikard, a student at Davidson College, began a discussion about the tension between owning one's domain and having the content on it graded by instructors.[11] Research is underway, at the time of writing, to examine the impact DoOO is having on pedagogy, student learning, and administrative practices.[12] There is much to untangle here, but remember, tangles are important when learning is involved.

TIP!

If you are interested in starting a local DoOO project at your institution or would like to start your own professional website, Reclaim Hosting is an option to help you get started. Reclaim Hosting is a company co-founded by Jim Groom and Tim Owens, who played integral roles in the development of the original DoOO project at University of Mary Washington. As explained on their website, the company "provides educators and institutions with an easy way to offer their students domains and web hosting that they own and control." Visit their site at ReclaimHosting.com to learn how to get started. Starting as an individual user with Reclaim Hosting is a great way to demonstrate the potential to your colleagues and start to change the teaching and learning paradigm at your own institution.

Rethinking the Textbook

The LMS isn't the only tool that is used pervasively in higher education. Nearly all college and university courses require students to purchase a textbook, which is a problem for several reasons. First, the cost of textbooks has risen astronomically in recent years. According to one study, their cost rose 73% between 2006 and 2016, which is four times the rate of inflation.[13] Moreover, research has shown that high textbook costs affect students' ability to achieve their academic goals. A 2012 report found that expensive textbooks are correlated with students taking fewer classes, dropping or withdrawing more frequently, and lower grades.[14] While many students are learning to take advantage of lower cost options through online textbook rental providers, high-risk, first-generation students are less likely than seasoned college students to be aware of these options and, thus, are impacted more. The situation is complex, but *no* evidence exists that shows high textbook costs are good for students.

In general, textbooks are valuable resources for faculty and students. They provide students with access to credible knowledge that pertains to a particular subject. They provide instructors with a structure for content. And often, textbooks come along with ancillary resources that may include presentation files aligned with the text's content, digital images replicating and enhancing the material in the book, and assessments. All of these resources are useful for faculty, as they may assist with developing a pathway for students to learn.

However, the content contained on the pages of the textbook and the ancillary materials are not owned by instructors. When instructors adopt a textbook for a course, they are licensed to use that content under certain conditions. In general, sharing the content with individuals not enrolled in the course is prohibited. Therefore, in order to continue to use the textbook and its subsequent editions, instructors who teach online or blended classes must ensure their instructional materials are secured within an environment that is only accessible to students enrolled in a course. *And there it is.* Our reliance on traditional textbooks works to reinforce our reliance on using an LMS.

There are various efforts underway to encourage faculty to create their own and/or adopt existing open educational resources (OER) in place of expensive commercial textbooks. An OER is any type of content (written text, video, image) that the copyright owner has chosen to share with a Creative Commons license (see Chapter 1 for more about open licenses and CC) or a work that resides in the public domain (has no copyright protection at all). Copyright owners can choose to share their work in the public domain (using a CC-0 license), but the main source is pre-1923 publications. (For a great selection of public domain works, go to HathiTrust.org, a consortium of university libraries). Using OER to reduce student textbook expenses seems like a simple solution. However, a study by the Babson Group found that most faculty members in higher education are unaware of OER, and they[15] cited many barriers to adopting to OER, including difficulty finding OER within particular disciplines.[16]

However, at the time of writing, efforts to educate faculty about OER and the problems associated with high textbook prices are underway. For example, public colleges and universities in California are designing campus-wide OER adoption efforts with funding from AB-798, California's College Textbook Affordability Act (for more info, go to Cool4ed.org). And community colleges across the nation are working with faculty who teach courses in high-demand degree programs to adopt OER, creating what are referred to as "Z-Degrees," short for "zero textbook costs."[17]

Replacing commercial content with OER does more, however, than reduce expenses for students. It also provides faculty with more options about how they teach their classes by eliminating the concerns about copyright violation. With OER, faculty and students are empowered to retain, re-use, revise, remix, and redistribute (see more about the 5Rs of OER later in this chapter) the content, which opens new opportunities for teaching, as well as learning.

Reducing the expense of textbook costs to students is just one reason to leverage OERs in one's teaching. However, Laura Gibbs, referenced earlier in this chapter, credits much of the creativity she integrates into her teaching to the public domain resources she locates and shares with her students. Gibbs does not use a textbook. Instead, she has spent time semester by semester, year by year, building a collection of myths and fables that are available online. These are stories that are no longer protected under copyright law because of the amount of time that has passed since the death of the author (United States copyright law is applicable for 70 years after the death of the author. If the work was a "work for hire," the term is even longer). For her Mythology and Folklore class, Gibbs has organized the stories into an "UN-textbook," which is presented to students in a blog format (MythFolklore.blogspot.com/). The stories are organized by themes into units, and the units are aligned with particular weeks in the class. For example, when a student clicks on the tab labeled "Weeks 2–3," they see Gibbs's instructions to select two units that interest them and read the stories linked below the unit's title. The unit options are Ancient Greece, Ancient Rome, From the Bible, Biblical Stores plus Apocrypha, Later Legends, or students may search for their own stories that align with these themes through additional links provided.

DEFINING THE "OPEN" IN OPEN CONTENT AND OPEN EDUCATIONAL RESOURCES (OER)

This material was created by David Wiley and published freely under a Creative Commons Attribution 4.0 license at OpenContent.org/definition/

The terms "open content" and "open educational resources" describe any copyrightable work (traditionally excluding software, which is described by other terms such as "open source") that is licensed in a manner that provides users with free and perpetual permission to engage in the 5R activities:

1. Retain—the right to make, own, and control copies of the content (e.g., download, duplicate, store, and manage)
2. Reuse—the right to use the content in a wide range of ways (e.g., in a class, in a study group, on a website, in a video)
3. Revise—the right to adapt, adjust, modify, or alter the content itself (e.g., translate the content into another language)
4. Remix—the right to combine the original or revised content with other material to create something new (e.g., incorporate the content into a mashup)
5. Redistribute—the right to share copies of the original content, your revisions, or your remixes with others (e.g., give a copy of the content to a friend)

OpenStax—Free High-Quality Textbooks

 OpenStax.org/higher-ed

Feature Overview

- A collection of free peer-reviewed textbooks authored by college and university faculty.
- All books shared with a CC license, providing the flexibility to support the 5R activities (listed earlier).
- Students may access the downloadable PDF and online versions at no cost; an iBook version is available for $5.00, and printed copies may also be purchased (at a very reduced rate compared to publisher textbooks).

OpenStax is a resource that may play a role in reducing the amount students spend each semester on their textbooks. A non-profit company based at Rice University and funded through philanthropic foundations, OpenStax provides free access to textbooks that have been through a rigorous peer-review process that rivals the same process used for commercial textbooks. OpenStax textbooks are written by subject-matter experts, shared with an open license, and peer-reviewed by subject mater experts.

SHOWCASE

OpenStax + Top Hat = Interactive Content and Engaged Learners

Joel Stake, a lecturer in biology at Louisiana Tech University, uses an OpenStax textbook for his Fundamentals of Biology I and II classes. His classes fall into the category of general education, and most of his students are non-biology majors. Biology textbooks are, in general, very expensive. My own quick Google search retrieved books that ranged from $70 to more than $200. Stake's use of the OpenStax textbook means that his students are not required to pay a penny for access to their book. His students may access the online version of the textbook or download it in PDF format for free (an accessible version that supports screen readers is also available). Students also have the option to pay $5.00 for the text in iBook format (viewable on iPads) and can choose to purchase a printed version of the book for $29.00. According to Stake's estimation, less than 1% of his students purchase a printed copy.

The OpenStax book that Stake uses is seasoned with a little something extra! It is one of the "interactive" textbooks offered by OpenStax that comes with Top Hat content baked inside. Top Hat, a separate company from OpenStax, offers an app that students download onto their mobile devices. By following simple instructions provided by their instructor, students use the app to respond to questions, polls, and more. By integrating Top Hat into the content of the OpenStax textbook, Stake has the opportunity to increase engagement in his classroom when the students are doing independent reading.

Stake's classes are large, enrolling more than 150 students each, which makes assessing student understanding extremely difficult in class. Upon reflection, Stake feels that using Top Hat has made him more conscientious of his students' learning. He explains, "In large enrollment classes it's too easy to just ask the class as a whole if they understand and then move on when no one asks a question. Silence doesn't equal understanding. Now I can see, based on their answers, if they are learning or if we need to go back through the material. I think that has been the biggest impact on me. I don't have to guess or assume they understand or don't understand. I can focus class time on the things that really need to be reinforced." It also serves as a handy way to take instant attendance!

In class, Stake displays his notes on the screen, but through the use of Top Hat, the notes are also visible directly on the students' devices. This process is effective, as Stake explains, because, ". . . if I want to modify the notes or annotate them in any way the students can see those changes in real time." He also embeds questions directly into the notes, providing students with opportunities to check in on their knowledge periodically during class. The student responses, Stake explains, "give me the opportunity to see how the class as a whole is doing based on the immediate feedback generated in Top Hat, but it also allows me later on to review each student's answers individually and identify students that may need more individual attention."

Outside of the classroom, Stake assigns reading from the OpenStax textbook and has students use Top Hat to respond to chapter questions. The student responses are usually counted toward class participation, but this type of formative assessment also gives learners and their instructor a chance to check in on progress over time. The knowledge that Stake gleans from the student responses helps him to determine the content that should be focused on in class. In this way, the Top Hat–infused OpenStax textbook is a handy flipped classroom strategy.

While the textbook itself is free, students pay about $25.00 for the Top Hat integration and an additional $5.00 for the integration of OpenStax into Top Hat (the student cost for Top Hat would be eliminated if Stake's institution had a site license for Top Hat). Stake shares, "I justify that by telling myself it is substantially cheaper than the average traditional biology textbook and far more useful, in my opinion." His students seem to agree. Stake notes that his students are very excited about the reduced cost compared to a traditional textbook, the immediate feedback Stake provides during the in-class Top Hat Q&A sessions, and how their class time is not spent on material that they've already mastered. The only drawback Stake identifies in using the OpenStax textbook is the attitude some individuals have about his text selection. He explains, "Sometimes people see it as an inferior resource, rather than what it really is, a viable alternative to traditional college textbooks."

Hypothes.is—Social Annotation on Web Pages

Hypothes.is

Feature Overview

- Free, open-source, non-profit tool for public discussion on the web.
- Annotation tool that enables note taking and critique on top of web pages.
- Annotations default to public, but options for keeping work private and working in groups is also available.
- Helpful "Teacher Resource Guide" includes getting started info and other tutorials.

Annotation has held a prevalent role in education for a very long time. When working with paper, it is a great way to engage students in critical analysis of essays and poems, research, discussions, and more. But what is the role of annotation on the web? Hypothes.is is a simple tool that allows any account holder to highlight text on any web page and insert one's own annotation. If you have a Hypothes.is account, all you need to do is install the Chrome extension and click on its icon in your browser's toolbar to launch the application. Once it is launched, any text that is annotated will appear highlighted in yellow. You may then click to expand the annotation toolbar, which displays all annotations for the page. You may add your own annotations or reply to any of the existing notes. The annotations may consist of text, image, or/and video.

By bringing annotation into the public and collaborative space of the web, annotations transform from text to a layer of rich media and open fascinating opportunities for teaching and learning, while fostering digital literacy skills. If you use Hypothes.is for a class activity and plan to have your students annotate multiple texts/sites, assign a hashtag and have your students include it in all of their annotations. All annotations that include the hashtag may be viewed in a simple activity stream by going to hypothes.is/stream and typing the hashtag into the search box.

At the time of writing, educators have begun using Hypothes.is in some very creative ways. A few examples are

- Elisa Beshero-Bondar of University of Pittsburgh-Greensburg uses Hypothes.is to facilitate scholarly annotation practice for her students.[18] To start, students select an online text from a resource list provided by their instructor. To claim the text as their own, students use Hypothes. is to mark a text with their own name. Each student carefully reads the text they have adopted and uses Hypothes.is to add supplementary and contextual information that serves to guide readers through the text. For example, Figure 6.2 shows an excerpt of A Ghost Story of Christmas by Charles Dickens (a public domain work available online through Project

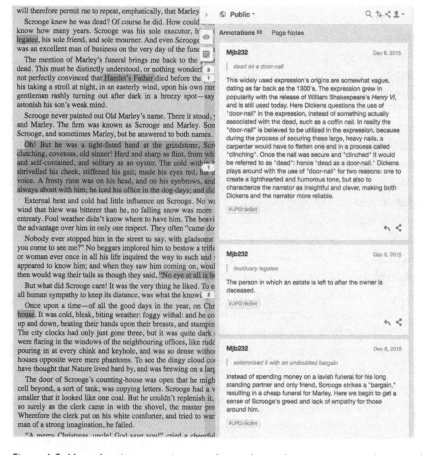

Figure 6.2 Hypothes.is annotations made on this website: www.gutenberg.org/files/46/46-h/46-h.htm#link1.

Gutenberg) on the left. If I launch Hypothes.is, I can view the annotations left by the student who claimed this work. The annotations line up with the highlighted text and guide me through the story by providing layers of context and explanations.

- Dr. Tony Fassi has his twelfth grade high school English class select a chapter of Moby Dick (from the Project Gutenberg site, where this public domain work is available online) and turn it into a "multimedia exhibit" by adding rich-media-based annotations to the online text. Students then present their exhibit to the class and record a five-minute overview of their project, which they upload to Sound Cloud.[19]

- Brian Watkins, a professor of anthropology at Austin College, uses Hypothes.is to have his students practice reading every day. His has simple and clear criteria for the students' annotations: for each reading assignment, every student must make three annotations. To receive credit, the annotations must demonstrate an action (questioning, commenting, answering, etc.), be constructive, be considerate of others' annotations, and be substantive in nature.[20]

 **TIP!**

Unsplash.com is a wonderful resource for locating high-resolution images that have been shared with a CC0 (Creative Commons Zero) license, which releases one's copyright of the work into the public domain. The images available for download on Unsplash may be modified and re-shared (even for commercial purposes) without permission or attribution.

Summary

We tend to view colleges and universities as institutions—a cluster of buildings, rooms, and public spaces through which faculty, administrators, staff, and students travel day-by-day and complete their individual tasks. But they're really ever-changing organizations that are intricately connected to the evolving world around us. As the web continues to alter the way our students live, learn, work, and socialize, the traditions that underpin teaching and learning in higher education must also change.

It is my hope that all of us in education today will see the importance of examining the changes occurring in the world beyond the edges of our campus and try our best to imagine stepping into the shoes of a student graduating and starting a job search. Building empathy for students is a powerful way to motivate ourselves to see our own traditions in a new light and to start conversations about making changes on campus. As you go about your meetings and planning sessions, think about your students and identify small ways you can contribute to diminishing the gap between the skills students *have* and the skills they *need* at graduation. There are amazing new practices taking shape in higher education, and many of them go entirely unrecognized, often because faculty feel too vulnerable to speak up and share what they're doing. Share your stuff (with an open license) and others will share back. Together, we can make change and empower our students to live productive, meaningful lives in the digital age.

Notes

1. Hill, P. (2014, September 15). LMS and Open: The False Binary Is Based on Past, Not Future Markets. *E-Literate Blog*. Retrieved on August 26, 2016 from http://mfeldstein.com/lms-open-false-binary-based-past-future-markets/.
2. Hill, P. (2014, September 17). Opening up the LMS Walled Garden. *E-Literate Blog*. Retrieved on August 26, 2016 from http://mfeldstein.com/opening-lms-walled-garden/.
3. Hill, P. & Feldstein, M. (2016). LMS Market Dynamics: Spring 2017 Edition. *MindWires LLC*, p. 5. Retrieved from www.mindwires.com.
4. Groom, J. & Lamb, B. (2014). Reclaiming Innovation. *EDUCAUSE Review Online*. Retrieved on August 18, 2016 from www.educause.edu/visuals/shared/er/extras/2014/ReclaimingInnovation/default.html.
5. Ross, J. & Collier, A. (2016). Complexity, Mess, and Non-yetness: Teaching Online with Emerging Technologies. In G. Veletsianos (Ed.), *Emergence and Innovation in Digital Learning* (pp. 17–33). Edmonton, AB: AU Press, Athabasca University.
6. Burtis, M. (2016, August 19). Making and Breaking Domain of One's Own: Rethinking the Web in Higher Ed. *Digital Pedagogy Lab*. Retrieved on August 23, 2016 from www.digitalpedagogylab.com/hybridped/making-breaking-rethinking-web-higher-ed.
7. Ibid.
8. Levine, A. (2013, January 28). Ds106: Not a Course, Not Like Any MOOC. *Educause Review*. Retrieved on August 26, 2016 from http://er.educause.edu/articles/2013/1/ds106-not-a-course-not-like-any-mooc.
9. Morgen, D. & Rorabaugh, P. (2014, January 28). Building Community and Critical Literacies with the Domain of One's Own Incubator. *Digital Pedagogy Lab*. Retrieved on August 28, 2016 from www.digitalpedagogylab.com/hybridped/building-community-critical-literacies-domain-ones-incubator/.
10. Ibid.
11. Rikard, A. (2015, August 10). Do I Own My Domain If You Grade It? *EdSurge*. Retrieved on August 26, 2016 from www.edsurge.com/news/2015–08–10-do-i-own-my-domain-if-you-grade-it.

12. Follow Pete Rorabaugh (http://peterorabaugh.org/), Lee Skallerup (http://readywriting.org/), who, at the time of writing, are both working on research projects related to DoOO. Also, the Division of Teaching and Learning Technologies at UMW blog at http://umwdtlt.com/dtlt-blog/has published a series of posts about the history of DoOO.

13. Senack, E. & Donogue, R. (2016). Covering the Cost. *Student Public Interest Research Groups*. Retrieved on July 26, 2016 from www.studentpirgs.org/reports/sp/covering-cost.

14. Donaldson, R. L., Nelson, D. W., & Thomas, E. (2012). 2012 Florida Student Textbook Survey. *Florida Virtual Campus*. Retrieved on July 26, 2016 from www.openaccesstextbooks.org/pdf/2012_Florida_Student_Textbook_Survey.pdf.

15. Straumshein, C. (2016, July 26). *Study Finds Use of Open Educational Resources on the Rise in Introductory Courses*. Retrieved on July 26, 2016, from www.insidehighered.com/news/2016/07/26/study-finds-use-open-educational-resources-rise-introductory-courses.

16. Allen, I. E. & Seaman, J. (2016). Opening the Textbook: Educational Resources in U.S. Higher Education, 2015–16. *Babson Survey Research Group*. Retrieved on July 26, 2016 from www.onlinelearningsurvey.com/reports/openingthetextbook2016.pdf.

17. *Lumen Learning*. Retrieved on August 26, 2016 from http://lumenlearning.com/oer-degree-programs/.

18. Beshero-Bondar, E. E. *Research Assignment: Scholarly Annotation*. Retrieved on August 26, 2016 from http://newtfire.org/19cBrit/AnnotResearchAssign.html.

19. Hypothesis. *Curate a Novel Chapter*. Retrieved on August 26, 2016 from https://hypothes.is/curate-a-novel-chapter/.

20. Hypothesis. *Annotation as a Reading "Action"*. Retrieved on August 26, 2016 from https://hypothes.is/annotation-as-a-reading-action/.

Chapter 7

Online Resources

Visit this book's online resource site: TeachingWithEmergingTech.com.

Like this book on Facebook: Facebook.com/BPTET.

On the online resources site, you will find a collection of resources aligned with each chapter in this book. The resources are compiled by the author from a variety of sources and are shared online, rather than in print, in an effort to ensure they are updated between editions.

If you are a Facebook user, please consider "Liking" this book's Facebook page. Doing so will show your support for the book, and you will also receive occasional updates from me in your Facebook feed about resources and articles related to the book's content. You are also welcome to message me directly through the Facebook page.

Finally, I encourage you to utilize the hashtag #BPTET and share your own online resources that relate to this book. This will allow me and anyone else to locate and view all related-web contributions by searching for the hashtag (unless the privacy settings for your account prohibit the content from being visible to the public). I hope that you will take this as an opportunity to experiment with hashtags and see how they work. This is a very useful strategy for your own teaching.

Here are a few ways you may contribute related content:

- Write a blog post containing a review of the book or a summary of your favorite takeaways.
- Take a photograph of yourself with the book and post it to Instagram, Facebook, or Twitter.
- Send a tweet that describes your favorite part of the book, a link to new tool that relates to one of the chapters, a practice you are going to try in your class, a new idea for a tool that others can learn from, or just to let me know you're reading it!

See you online!

Michelle

@brocansky

Index